Praises for

Hope Abides

Horrific things happen to good people without rational explanation. Charlotte lost her entire family in a plane crash. On April 1, 1990, I lost my wife Ellen, my entire family, in a car crash. We had been married for seventy-seven days. Charlotte and I are both Christians, and we both struggled to understand how the "kind and just" God we had been taught to believe in and trust could allow us to be hurt so badly. Through all the tears, anger, and relapses that were triggered when a special song came on the radio, we both realized God loved us by putting Larry, Landon, and Ellen in the center of our lives. *Hope Abides: My Journey Through Grief* in NOT a step-by-step instruction book to overcome unbearable grief. Instead, Charlotte's book clearly shows the only true path forward from despair is faith in God. Please read and believe.

—Pete Olson, United States Congressman
Texas Congressional District 22
2009 - 2021

***

Charlotte Liptack has done the impossible - she fully and wholly describes grief in all of it brutal entirety. As a mother who has lost a child I never thought it possible to describe the pain - not just the emotional and mental agony, but the actual *physical* pain - but she absolutely nails it. And while she reminds us that losing a spouse makes us a widow and losing a parent makes us an orphan, there is no word for a parent who loses a child. But if there ever is such a word, Charlotte Liptack will be the one to invent it.

—**Kathie Truitt**, author "False Victim" (Lifetime Movie) The Neighbor in the Window

***

Hope Abides: My Journey Through Grief is an incredibly open and honest book filled with the real emotions and genuine faith of Charlotte Liptack's survival journey. Liptack's strength and vulnerability allows readers to understand the stages of grief and the healing process when faced with tragic loss. The importance of a strong dependence on faith is evident throughout. This book will have a life long impact on everyone who reads it.

—**Koda Martin**, NFL Offensive Lineman, Former Student

***

In *Hope Abides: My Journey Through Grief,* Charlotte bravely takes us along on a journey; one that is filled with love, pain, healing, and in the end a perfect peace that surpasses all understanding. This book gives insight into the story of a woman who experienced debilitating pain through an unimaginable loss, and with her love of God battled her way through the devastation of losing a husband and a child and discovered how to live again. Reading this book will allow the reader to take this journey with Charlotte and understand that healing is possible, even when it seems as if the pain will never subside. Through tragedy, Charlotte's purpose was revealed, and with this book she reminds us that with God's promises, we too can find peace. There is no doubt in my mind that the experiences shared in this book will help someone make it through the most difficult time in their life and know that they are not alone.

—**Tomika Gamble**, MD Anderson Program Manager, Pediatrics

***

Charlotte bravely and courageously shares her experiences of tremendous loss, grief, faith, and hope. She shares the personal steps she has taken as she continues to find freedom in the rough waters of life. I believe this world is a better place because of our shared stories of hope. She says, "true HOPE is an absolute faith and certainty of God and His promises." I know without a shadow of a doubt that God's promises are true. I also know that Charlotte's story can be used by God to make a difference in the life of someone who is hurting.

—**Toby Slough**, Founder of Goby International Ministries & Founder and Legacy Pastor of Cross Timbers Church

***

As I sat in the church the day of the memorial service I wondered, "how can one person deal with such a tragedy?" This book details the "how." All of the emotions and faith that one can have is chronicled in this book, the journey of a tragedy. Charlotte's faith and love prevails.

—**Ed Thompson,** Texas State Representative

Hope Abides

My Journey Through Grief

Charlotte Liptack

Published by KHARIS PUBLISHING, imprint of KHARIS MEDIA LLC.

Copyright © 2022 Charlotte Liptack

ISBN-13: 978-1-63746-125-9
ISBN-10: 1-63746-125-9
Library of Congress Control Number: 2022935560

Unless otherwise indicated, all Scripture quotations are from the New King James Version Copyright 1982 by Thomas Nelson, Inc.

Scripture taken from THE HOLY BIBLE, NEW INTERNATIONAL VERSION ®. Copyright© 1973, 1978, 1984, 2011 by Biblica, Inc.™. Used by permission of Zondervan

All KHARIS PUBLISHING products are available at special quantity discounts for bulk purchase for sales promotions, premiums, fund-raising, and educational needs. For details, contact:

Kharis Media LLC
Tel: 1-479-599-8657
support@kharispublishing.com
www.kharispublishing.com

Hope Abides: My Journey Through Grief is dedicated to my stepdaughters Lauren and Juliet. They too lost a part of their heart that day; they lost their dad and brother. Lauren and Juliet have taught me so much about grace, forgiveness and HOPE. They have loved and embraced me in a way I never could have imagined and blessed me with beautiful grandchildren. I love you both to the moon and back "emillion times," as your brother would say.

Contents

Foreword

We have this HOPE as an anchor for the soul, firm and secure.

Hebrews 6:19-20

This is the story of my survival journey after losing my nine-year-old son and only child and my husband of 19 years in one event on a single day. I call it "survival" because there were times I thought I might die from a broken heart. Although God has traveled with me on this journey, it has not been pretty. I have begged God to let me wake up from the nightmare. I have cursed God. I have called Him a liar, told Him that this was not love, and that He had crossed the line. I've also fallen on my knees and cried out for mercy.

I have begged Him to take me home to Heaven, as well, and threatened to take my own life. All the while, God stood beside me. He was and is big enough, holy enough, sovereign enough and forgiving enough to hold me through all my doubt and anger. There were so many times that I couldn't even utter a word or prayer. I would simply sit and cry. Time after time in my moments of deepest despair, God was there. I could hear the whisper of His promises, I could feel the comfort of His arms holding me, I could see His miracles all around me in the moon, the stars, the sunset, and the sunrise. I have asked God *why* over a thousand times. I have not yet heard His answer. All I do know is, God's ways are not my ways, that He has a plan bigger than me, this life, and this world. One day, when I get to Heaven, I will understand, however, on that glorious day, I doubt it will matter much.

When I lost my son and husband, I looked for other, similar survival stories to help me on my journey. I couldn't find any regarding losing a child or child and spouse. My prayer is that my story brings you comfort, peace, and will help you as you travel your survival journey.

01
Chapter

My Crazy, Not So Perfect Life

I grew up in what was once the small town of Mansfield, just outside Fort Worth, TX. I was one of five sisters. We grew up in a two-parent Christian home. Things weren't always pretty at home, but Mom's faith was strong, and she had us in church every time the doors were open.

We often lived in the rooms of the hotels Dad managed. I remember one somewhat sketchy hotel in Arlington. The five of us lived in the two rooms. We often ate dinner in the cafe attached to the hotel. Once a week, as a treat, we got to indulge in chocolate milk and vending machine honey buns. We would run to the machine, get a honey bun to split, then run over to the cafe for chocolate milk. We would take it back to our room, snuggle up in our pajamas, and eat in bed. This ritual is such a vivid memory from my childhood. Obviously, it wasn't the extraordinary, culinary delectable that make it so memorable; I assume it has something to do with the feeling of comfort. In all those chaotic moments of life in hotels, in those moments curled up with my sister in the hotel bed, we almost felt normal. In our childhood minds, this is what we thought home was supposed to feel like. When I was about eight we moved to New Mexico. Again, we lived in a hotel but this time it was different. This hotel had a large, two-bedroom suite and sat perched atop two spiral staircases in the hotel lobby. Although simple, my sisters and I felt like princesses walking down those staircases. I distinctly remember it had a kitchen. Not that we hadn't had a kitchen before, but it had been a while. A kitchen meant chocolate milk every night. I distinctly remember pouring cold glasses of milk for me and my sisters and then popping open the metal can of chocolate mix and stirring until our bedtime treat was ready.

In all this moving around, the thread that constantly followed was abuse. When Dad was mad or frustrated, he took his aggressions out on us. Older sisters took the brunt of the physical abuse while my younger sisters took the pain of the verbal abuse with its scars. Many times, the bruises had to be covered for days or even weeks but the emotional scars can never fade.

Dad was injured in a serious work accident when I was just 10 years old. Not long after that, Mom went to work for the first time to put food on the table. A year later, the house caught fire. It seemed like there was one tragedy after another. Mom and Dad spent most of my childhood scraping by. The Baptist church was how my family survived. The church put food on the table, they helped pay the bills, they visited when Dad was in the hospital; they provided the Christmas gifts we opened; they were our community.

I was the first in my family to go to college. I attended Howard Payne University, a private Baptist college in Brownwood, TX, where I met and married my first husband. For reasons too numerous to list, that marriage ended four years later. This was something Baptist girls didn't do. I was shamed by my family, my friends, and especially my church. I struggled to survive those painful years alone.

About the time I finished my teaching degree, I met Larry. He was my true soulmate. I saw him as my rescuer. He saved me from the judgment of divorce. He rescued me from a life of abuse. He was my everything and he helped me feel complete. We dated for a few years and were married on June 29, 1995. We were truly the best of friends. We laughed together, played together, skipped work together, traveled together, and chased our dreams together. One of the highlights of our marriage was spending as much time as possible on our boat. Her name was Satistaction, which we kept on Clear Lake, just off Galveston Bay. We would wake up in the morning, sit on the back of the boat, me with a cup of coffee and Larry with a Coke™ and just listen to the waves lap against the hull. We would take weekend trips on our boat, and every summer when my teaching year was over, we would take an extended trip for two weeks to a month on our boat. We loved our life together and were making the most of it; I couldn't imagine anything being more perfect.

Larry had often talked of flying. He had started training for his pilot's license but had never finished. One year for his birthday, I purchased his flight school tuition, and thus began new adventures. We flew all over the country and Caribbean. We loved flying back and forth to the Bahamas. Larry's two girls, Lauren and Juliet, from his previous marriage loved flying with him as well. He frequently flew to Dallas to see them or pick them up for the weekend. Our lives seemed pretty perfect.

We were living in Deer Park, TX when, in March 2004, I learned I was pregnant. On November 18, 2004, our lives were complete. We had Landon, the perfect gift. I never knew I could experience more love. I held him endlessly. I would sneak into his room at night, pick him up and hold him for hours while he slept. As he grew, I fell more in love each day. Larry began to travel a lot for work, so it was often just Landon and me at home. He and I had a bond that was special. He used to curl up next to me on the couch and say, "Mom, you and me are in love." He was right. I was in love but he was a daddy's boy through and through. He was all about Mom until Dad walked in the door, then it was boy time. They played for hours every day. When Landon was young, he and Larry would spend hours lining up Matchbox™ toy cars, motorcycles, and airplanes for various races around the house. Sometimes they would gang up on Mom in Nerf™ gun wars, claiming boys rule the house. As Landon grew older, their time together was baseball, time at the hangar, or riding motorcycles. They couldn't get enough of each other, and I couldn't get enough of them. I had it all. For the first time in my life, I truly felt my cup running over with what God called blessings. I didn't know if I truly deserved all that God had given me, but I was doing my part to honor Him and cherish every moment with my boys. Life was picture perfect in my eyes. I was totally in love and had never felt more loved than I did by my boys.

There is a time for everything, and a season for every activity under the Heavens: A time to be born and a time to die, a time to plan and a time to uproot, a time to kill and a time to heal, a time to tear down and a time to build, a time to week and a time to laugh, a time to mourn and a time to dance, a time to scatter stones and a time to gather them, a time to embrace and a time to refrain from embracing, a time to search and a time to give up, a time to keep and a time to throw away, a time to tear and a time to mend, a time to be silent and a time to speak, a time to love and a time to hate, a time for war and a time for peace.

Ecclesiastes 3:1-8

02
Chapter

The Phone Call That Changed My Life

When Landon was about three years old, I got a call from my previous boss and longtime friend, Darrell. He had opened a new high school in the Alvin ISD, TX and wanted me to come back to work for him as his head counselor. I laughed and told him I loved being a stay-at-home mom. I finally joked and told him that if he would hire me part-time and put a crib in the office next door, I would come back to work. Boy, did I eat my words! The next day he called to say the district had approved my part-time status. Although there would be no crib next door, I would be able to work two-and-a-half days per week while Landon was in childcare at the neighborhood church. Little did I know, that was the beginning of God putting a plan in motion. Not my plan, but His, and not only would it be my saving grace, it saved my life.

I continued working as a part-time school counselor for the next two years and those years would begin to shape my philosophy as a school principal and district administrator. I also began working with dear friends during this time, the kind of friends one will call family. I had just started my third year as a school counselor at the high school when my boss asked me to take an assistant principal position. I remember chuckling as I reminded him I wasn't qualified to be an assistant principal. A few months later, I finished my principal's certification and began a new career as a school administrator. I moved quickly through the ranks and became an associate principal a year and a half later.

Two years later, a position as a junior high principal opened in the district. By all accounts, the job would be mine. I was the most qualified. However, God had bigger plans. After bombing the interview, the committee told me they were moving in another direction. I remember my boss asking me what had happened and what I said. He just couldn't understand and neither could I; it was devastating. That may have been the first time in my career I hadn't gotten a promotion I had applied for. What I did know was that I loved working at the high school, I loved my boss, I loved the kids, and I would enjoy every moment of the job I did have.

A year later, my boss got a promotion, leaving the position of principal of Manvel High School open. It was unusual to take a sitting associate principal and move them into that position. Most likely, according to history, a sitting junior high principal would get the job. However, I knew no one loved that campus more than I did. No one could do a better job. Against all odds, I applied. Three weeks later I was named principal of Manvel High School. My boss and friend Darrell told me that I had one opportunity to stand in front of my staff for the first time and make an impression as their new leader. I took that seriously. My staff knew me as their associate principal, but I had been leading under someone else's vision. I wanted them to know my heart, my reasons, my vision. As I prepared for that first day of in-service as principal, I knew I wanted to share my story as a child in school and how one administrator had changed my life. That day was tough, however, because my story wasn't easy to tell. My past had been riddled with abuse and that day, as I told my story, there wasn't a dry eye in the room. As I shared my past, I won the hearts of 200-plus staff members. We bonded that day in a new way. They knew the importance of their relationships with kids. They also knew that if that was first, then there wasn't anything they couldn't accomplish with kids. We did amazing things that first year. I had a staff I adored who worked hard for kids, I spent hours loving on kids myself, and in the end, there wasn't anything we wouldn't do for one another. We had become a true family.

My husband and son, Larry and Landon, had decided to take a "boys' trip" to see Grandma, Larry's mom in Bowie, TX. It was the weekend before school would start and a perfect time to get a way. Larry picked up Landon from a friend's house on Thursday. We met at home. They packed a bag and headed to the sailboat to spend the night. This was our happy place. Without fail, we spent the weekend on our sailboat on Clear Lake, near Houston. I didn't go that weekend. I was working the next day, and they were leaving to see Grandma. I called about 9pm and they had just returned from seeing a movie. The next morning, we talked again. They were going to wash the boat, have Chick-Fil-A™ for breakfast, head to the airport, and wash the plane before heading to Bowie. Once more that morning, they asked if I wanted to go. I declined... a decision I often regret.

It was August 15, 2014, the Friday before school started. I was working hard to prepare for that second year as principal and for teachers to return to school that next Monday. Looking back, I distinctly remember thinking, *My whole life is in that plane.* I had that thought often, as they loved to fly and this was regular practice.

About 4pm that day, I received a call that would forever change my life. My mother-in-law was on the other end and said, "Charlotte, the plane has gone down!"

Vaguely, I remember what happened next. Suddenly, there was this noise I couldn't identify at first. It was loud and overwhelming. I couldn't breathe. It was an unusual noise, a noise of hurt, pain, and agony. I couldn't quite figure it out. It took a while before I realized that the shrillness I was hearing was my own. I fell to the floor as staff members ran in trying to figure out what was happening. It wasn't long before I lay surrounded by dear friends, the kind of friends you call family. Right in that moment, everything I had worked hard to create, the relationships I had built, came full circle and held me as I began to navigate all that was happening.

I kept asking questions. I refused to believe it was possible. I lay there repeating, "NO, NO, NO, NO!" Denial set in. I refused to accept this fate. I jumped up and started calling airports, other pilots, anyone who could verify that it just wasn't true. I couldn't find answers. My friend and associate principal Raymond was in the room with me when I received the call. Debbie, my secretary and friend, stayed by my side. It wasn't long before my dearest friends, Darrell, Shawn and Leslie, were all surrounding me. I still refused to accept this fate.

Not long afterward, I was loaded into a car and taken to my home. More and more people arrived. Someone quickly took away my cell phone. Helicopters began to circle the house and the news crews started swarming the yard. More and more people arrived. They crowded the living room. If I went to my room, they followed. People were everywhere. At some point food began to arrive. It was enough food to feed the crowd that had formed. People would walk around me, there was a humming of whispers all around the room. Few felt comfortable enough to engage in conversation with me. Some people kept asking me if I wanted to go lie down. *No,* I thought. *I must find my husband and child. Where are they? Why haven't I heard any updates? This cannot be them.*

About an hour later, someone handed me my cell phone. My mom and four sisters were on the line. I sat surrounded by friends, with my family on speaker phone, and listened as my dear friend Shawn sat across from me. He would confirm my worst nightmare. The police had confirmed that Larry and Landon were indeed on the plane that had crashed. They had not survived; they had died August 15, 2014.

Cries of devastation again escaped my body. I had no control. The cries poured out of me as if they were asking someone to please relieve the pain. All I could think was that I could not do this. I could not and did not want to try. I just wanted to be with my husband and child. Later that night, my mom and sisters arrived and I again lost all control. Their arrival made it more real. They wouldn't have been there, 300 hundred miles from home, if it weren't something tragic or significant. "No, no, no, I can't do this, I don't want to do this," I cried. Shortly after family arrived, the friends who had gathered began to depart. That night, a friend brought over medication; it was the type of medication meant to knock me out and let me sleep and escape this nightmare. I don't know what it was, only that one of my sisters told me to take it. My family huddled around me and held me until I fell asleep and, for a brief time, escaped the horror and pain of that living nightmare; in the early morning hours I woke to the painful reality once again.

The immediate devastation and shock of it all was so overwhelming. I couldn't breathe, I couldn't stop the uncontrollable crying. A fear so real, so big, and so daunting began to consume me like a dark cloud covering every aspect of my life. I kept thinking and saying over and over, "I can't do this; I don't want to do this." All the while God kept whispering:

Yea though I walk through the valley of the shadow of death, I will fear no evil: for thou art with me; thy rod and thy staff they comfort me.

Psalms 23:4

October 12, 2014

It's been almost two months since that dreadful day. The day I received the call that would forever change my life...

It was August 15, 2004 at about 4:30 - 5:00 pm. I was sitting in my office working preparing for the following weeks teacher inservice.
The phone (cell) rang. It was Judy, Larry's mom. She was crying. "The plane went down", she cries. That moment, those words forever changed me. I dropped the phone and began to scream, "No God!

Delight yourself in the LORD
and He will give you the desires of your heart.
Psalm 37:4

Please God. Please don't let them die....

August 14th My husband and son decided to have a boys weekend. They went to a movie "Guardians of the Galaxy", ate dinner and went to spend the night on the boat. The next morning they decided to get in the new plane and head to Bowie to visit Larry's mom & Landon's grandma, Judy. About a mile north of the airport the plane crashed and exploded into a fiery inferno My whole world was on that Plane. Larry, my husband of 19 years and Landon my

The LORD is my light and my salvation – whom shall I fear?
The LORD is the stronghold of my life – of whom shall I be afraid?
Psalm 27:1

only child of 9 years, died that day. That day still haunts me. The call still plays in my head. I still long for them to walk back in the door so I can hold them again. It to been a difficult two months but God has began to heal my broken heart and give me a peace that passes all understanding.

The LORD Himself goes before you and will be with you;
He will never leave you nor forsake you.
Deuteronomy 31:8

03
Chapter

The Haze

The morning after the accident, Saturday, my sisters and mom loaded me into a car and took me back to Fort Worth. The accident had happened just outside of Fort Worth. I knew I would need to be in that area for the next few days as details were sorted out. Most of that car ride I sat motionless in the backseat with my head propped against the window. The panic attacks would come and go, leaving me crying and gasping for air. The tears flowed freely, as if I couldn't ever stop crying; it was constant and unrelenting.

I can only describe what I experienced those first few days as being in a state of psychological shock. There were two distinct levels of awareness: In one state, I cried continually. The realization of my loss was just too much to handle. I couldn't manage a thought, a need, or even a word;

I simply wept. The other state was different. I was numb and felt like I was outside my own body, I felt nothing. This state was my body's and mind's way of surviving. It was how I coped with sitting in front of Larry's children, my stepdaughters. It was how I made funeral arrangements; it was how I listened to the NTSB tell me about the plane crash.

Sleep was my only escape from the pain but it came in such short stints. I was exhausted yet couldn't calm my mind enough to sleep. At the same time, I craved sleep. When I slept, I wasn't aware of the reality of my situation.

I was also keenly aware of this constant tightness or weight on my chest but I couldn't figure out what it was. It was heavy and constricting, often leaving me gasping for air. I felt like I couldn't catch my breath. Sometimes I would breathe so hard I hyperventilated. I would have to put my head between my knees and breathe into a paper bag just to make it through the days.

On Monday morning, we went to the funeral home to make arrangements. This was something I had never done, something a spouse and mom should never have to do. I had always imagined my first experience in that room would be to plan a funeral for a parent, not my child. The room was packed with family. Again, that survival shock kicked in. I spoke in monotone, asking my stepdaughters how we should proceed. They were too devastated, so I began to make decisions for which I had never prepared.

Charlotte Liptack

Due to the nature of the accident, the crash, the explosion, and the fire, Larry and Landon would be cremated, and their ashes put in a shared box inscribed with their names. There would be two memorial services, one in Fort Worth in my mom's church, where most of our family continued to reside, and the second service in our hometown church in Manvel, TX, where we had made so many friends over the last 20 years.

I have only short clips of memories from those two memorial services. It's as if my mind created a video and only saved a few short clips. In the first service, I remember my boss, Superintendent Fred Brent, coming to sit next to me. He wrapped his arm around me and told me I was one of the strongest women he knew. I hardly felt strong at that point, as the only thing I could do was cry. From the second service, I only have a few memories. I remember Landon's three young friends, eight and nine years old, taking the stage and speaking about their memories of Landon. I remember thinking they were so innocent before this happened; they were too young to be engaging in such an experience. My other memory was after the memorial service, looking up to see hundreds of Manvel HS students in their various uniforms lined up to wrap their arms around me. I didn't know a principal could be so loved.

Tuesday, the day after making funeral arrangements, the NTSB came to talk. I remember, in strange detail, the moment I sat in the living room with my family, my two stepdaughters, and Larry's mom and heard the gentleman from the NTSB talk about the crash and the process that lay ahead. Strangely, I couldn't hear some of what he was saying, yet I was keenly aware of everything. It was as if the sound would fade in and out throughout the conversation. He was looking directly at me and talking. When I could hear him, the things he said made my eyes well up with tears so I couldn't see anything but the fuzzy images of family all around. He discussed how difficult the accident scene had been for the first responders, saying that several of them were dads and they grieved with me. He then began to describe the process of taking the plane apart and moving to a hangar and reassembling the airplane. This would enable them to find any problems and try to detect what happened that dreadful day. Then his voice would fade into a continuous dull hum, as if coming from so far away. In those moments, I looked around the room at Larry's mom, who sat as motionless as I had been. My gaze moved then to my two stepdaughters, who sat with their heads hanging down in disbelief. They occasionally moved their gaze from the NTSB investigator, to me, and back to the floor. In these moments, I sat and thought of the future, *How would we survive, what the future would look like? Would we all stay connected? How would we move from one moment to the next?* In those moments, it was as if I were watching from above. Then, in the same way the NTSB officer's voice faded, it would slowly become audible again.

I remember him telling me that the plane had been engulfed in flames and there was nothing left except Larry's wedding band and a bag in the forward compartment. He would have that bag delivered in a few days. He talked about how strange it was that the bag wasn't damaged, as if it somehow had been protected.

A few days later, there was a knock at the door. It was a delivery from the NTSB. I became paralyzed with fear about what I might find in that box. It sat unopened until my sister arrived and checked the contents. When I opened the box, I was shocked. It was Landon's baseball bag, which with the contents inside had miraculously escaped the flames. Inside I found Landon's cleats, bat, baseballs, and both his and Larry's gloves. They had loved playing ball together and played every chance they had. It was never just a game of catch. There were bases, a pitcher's mound, and every hit scored a run. It was a baseball game. I loved watching them play. At that moment, I knew exactly how that bag had survived...God. God had protected that bag to send me a message. At that moment, I knew as well that they were in God's hands. I knew they were safe from all harm just like that bag had been protected. I knew God was telling me that they were together. It was my miracle in the chaos and tragedy.

My eyes have grown dim with grief, my whole frame is but a shadow.

Job 17:7

When I said, "My foot is slipping," your unfailing love, Lord, supported me.

Psalms 94:18

October 13, 2014

I must have been in shock. I remember so little of the next two weeks except for parts of the Dallas memorial and all of the Houston memorial. I kept expecting to wake up from a bad dream, but everyday I woke up to the reality that my husband and child were gone. I've cried every day since. Sometimes all day and uncontrollably. I wish often that this nightmare would end and I too would die just so I can see them again.

I remember the last conversation with both of

them. Thursday night I called and talked to Landon. He told me about the movie. He told me he and dad were going to play baseball at Grandma's house. That was the last time I ever heard his voice. I still remember him saying, "I Love you, mom." "I love you too", I replied.

The next day I talked to Larry. He was going to airport. He and Landon were flying to his moms. He asked if I wanted to go. I told him I needed to stay & work. I've regretted that moment ever since. I wish I had been on that plane. I wish I had been

I can do everything through Him who gives me strength.
Philippians 4:13

38

been with them i their last moments. I wish I had died that day with them.

How does one go on after such a catastrophic loss? What do I do? How do I live? How do I cope? Nothing feels normal. I couldn't eat for the 1st 3 weeks & couldn't sleep. Doctors prescribed Zoloft and Lunesta. So now I sleep and survive each day. I feel lost and without purpose without them here. My whole world revolved around being a mom & having a happy family. We were so happy, so perfect, so in love, all having so much fun... until that Crash!

If you want to know what God wants you to do —
ask Him, and He will gladly tell you.
James 1:5

04
Chapter

Cries

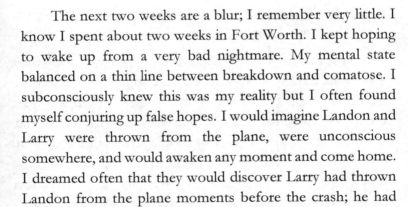

The next two weeks are a blur; I remember very little. I know I spent about two weeks in Fort Worth. I kept hoping to wake up from a very bad nightmare. My mental state balanced on a thin line between breakdown and comatose. I subconsciously knew this was my reality but I often found myself conjuring up false hopes. I would imagine Landon and Larry were thrown from the plane, were unconscious somewhere, and would awaken any moment and come home. I dreamed often that they would discover Larry had thrown Landon from the plane moments before the crash; he had survived and was searching for me. I often thought this was truly a vivid nightmare and I would awaken only to hold them again. Nothing made any sense to me.

I didn't eat those first two weeks and drank only when told. I couldn't sleep. Most of the time, I couldn't breathe because of the weight on my chest. I could do nothing but cry. Doctors prescribed antidepressants, anti-anxiety meds and a sleep aid and that allowed me to sleep a few hours each night and to make it through the next day. I felt so lost and without purpose. My purpose in life was being a mom and wife. *We were so happy, so perfect, so in love, and all having the times of our lives. What would be my purpose now? What would I do? How would I survive without them? My whole heart was gone?*

During those first two weeks, I often thought of that last conversation. It was a Thursday night and the boys, as I referred to them, had decided to spend the night on the sailboat. They went out to eat and to a movie. Landon told me all about the movie and that they had their baseball stuff so they could play at Grandma's. I still remember hearing him say, "I love you, Mom." And I replied, "I love you too."

That next morning I talked to Larry. They were on their way to the airport. They were heading to Bowie, TX to have a little time away before school started. Larry asked one more time if I wanted to go. I told him no, that I needed to stay and work. I have regretted that moment, that decision, a lot. Had I gone, I would have been with them in their last moments. I could have assured Larry that it was all ok. I could have comforted my little boy and held him tight. I would not have been left to survive in all the pain.

Grief has so many stages. Mine started with denial, but hopelessness was just around the corner. In those first two weeks I held on to denial, imagining, as I said, that just before the crash they had been thrown from the plane and were lying unconscious in a hospital somewhere. They would soon wake up and we would be reunited. My mind would play horrible tricks; I would think I heard one of them call out to me, and I would wake from sleep thinking I heard a door open, then run down the hall, only to find the hallway empty. These moments only strengthened my denial.

The exhaustion of grief began to set in during those first two weeks. I had no energy; I had used all my energy to weep uncontrollably. My body was physically and emotionally drained. All I could do was cry. I cried all day; I cried all night. Although I had begun to feel utterly helpless, I knew I needed to cry out to God. I knew He was my only hope in surviving. Yet the prayers wouldn't come.

I felt I existed those first two weeks as though I was walking on the edge of a cliff. I balanced there, often knowing that at any moment I could lose control and fall into an uncontrollable sob. One evening, I had been living on that edge all day long, as tears streamed down my cheeks at the thought of Larry and Landon. All day there was a lump in my throat that wouldn't go away. I was on the brink of a meltdown. I decided I needed to step away, hide for a while, and just allow myself to fall apart.

My only safe space then was the bathroom; I slipped in and turned on the music and water just in time to fall apart. I lay on the bathroom floor for what seemed like hours. I cried and cried. I tried so hard to pray. The only words that would come were, "Why? WHY GOD WHY?" At one such moment, I thought of David. I remembered that throughout scripture David often cried out to God for mercy and for peace. I tried again to pray, "Jesus…." and then more crying. "Jesus," I bellowed and then more crying. On and on it went for at least thirty minutes. "Jesus," I sobbed between breaths. "Jesus," I sobbed and gasped for air. "Jesus," I wailed uncontrollably and loud, over and over, uttering His name until finally my sobbing quieted and my breathing began to slow.

That night, Jesus met me on the bathroom floor and held me; He held me until I could feel His presence and breathe again. In the end, I was soaked with sweat, covered in snot and tears, exhausted, shaking, but I truly believe my Heavenly Father held me in that moment when no one else could. So when I started sobbing uncontrollably again, I would simply repeat His name until I could breathe again and the cries subsided. Every time, my Heavenly Father was faithful to relieve the acute anxiety attacks when the only word or thought I could form was, "Jesus, Jesus, Jesus."

God, my family, and closest friends, were how I survived those first few weeks. They never left my side. They slept beside me, sat beside me, held me, fed me… I'm so thankful for them. I'm thankful they didn't give me the choice but to be carried by them.

Evening, morning and noon I cry out in distress, and he hears my voice.

Psalms 55:17

Though he brings grief, he will show compassion, so great is his unfailing love.

Lamentations 3:32

October 14, 2014

    Today was a rough day. I'm not sure why but I cried all day. The grief came on like a big wave; a tsunami. It covered me and I couldn't find my way out. I thought of my little Landon and how much I miss hearing his voice and kissing his face. I thought about Larry and how much I miss his warmth, companionship, and security. There was nothing he couldn't do. I know he could handle every situation. I worry about Lauren + Juliet + Judy. However, I can hardly care

If anyone is in Christ, he is a new creation;
the old has gone, the new has come!
2 Corinthians 5:17

for myself. How can I help them through their grief. I feel so obligated and responsible yet helpless.

I'm trying not to fear what lies ahead. Nothing could be worse than this. But so much looms...

the investigation, is there a wrongful death?, insurance, life insurance, bills, taxes... There is so much to do....

Tonight I will pray for peace, rest, comfort and one day joy — it seems impossible but I'm resting on Gods promises. I know He is faithful to His word.

Cast your cares on the LORD and He will sustain you.
Psalm 55:22

05
Chapter

A Physical Response to Grief

Although I knew that our bodies physically react to stress, I didn't know our bodies grieved. I could never have imagined the physical pain I would endure in grieving. As a counselor, I knew that there were psychological and emotional responses to grief, however, I didn't know there were physical responses to grief, as well. I couldn't think; I couldn't sleep; I couldn't eat, and I couldn't speak. I only knew how to cry. I think traumatic shock must have set in shortly after hearing the news and I believe it's the mind's way of self-preservation.

What happened those first two to three weeks I can only describe as a breakdown, physically, mentally, and emotionally. I kept complaining that I couldn't breathe, there was a tightness, pain, and contraction that I felt with every breath. Now, I know it was anxiety, but then, when I couldn't catch my breath, I wondered if I was having a heart attack, if I was dying of a broken heart.

Yes, the body physically grieves too. My physical reaction to grief was like nothing I had ever experienced. I noticed that my body was in extreme pain. Every single muscle and joint ached. I had been so tense and was contracting every muscle in my body for so long that I felt as if I was on fire at times. The pain felt somewhere between the pain after an extreme workout and being in a bad car accident. It hurt to sit, it hurt to move, it hurt to sleep, I just hurt.

A friend of mine, a chiropractor, Angel Keng, was my true angel. She suggested I come in. She and I spent some time talking and she recommended I come for treatment every few days for a while. She started with light adjustments and then her therapist would do some light massages. Although painful, it helped tremendously. I'm pretty sure I cried through every adjustment and massage. I did this every two to three days for about three weeks. Slowly my body began to relax, the pain subsided, and my body began to heal.

Another thing I noticed was that my skin became sensitive to touch. It was as if I had been sunburned. The sensitivity made me hesitant to be hugged or touched. It was as if my body was grieving the loss of those warm hugs from my son and husband. Just as if I were sunburned, the skin all over my body peeled off. It was a strange reaction, but the more I read the more I began to understand that emotional stress can physically manifest itself in a variety of ways. This physical reaction made me withdraw even more. I simply refused touch. I covered my skin, wore long sleeves and long pants, and didn't allow others to hug me. I was so used to wrapping my arms around Landon every single day that I didn't know how to survive without hugging him. It manifested itself in wanting to withdraw from all human touch. It doesn't seem at all rational, yet all I knew was that if I couldn't hug my boys, I didn't want to hug anyone, nor want anyone to hug me.

I constantly felt nauseous and still couldn't eat. I rarely drank anything and became dehydrated more than once during those first several months. Not eating was one thing, but not drinking water was another. The dehydration was awful and may very well have been the cause of some of my physical symptoms. The stomach cramps, headaches, and exhaustion that came from dehydration were another complication I just couldn't handle and it added an unnecessary amount of stress.

As exhausted as I felt, I continued struggling to find sleep. Although it was my only reprieve from the emotional pain, I couldn't fall asleep or stay asleep. My mind simply raced. It wasn't long before I had to consult my doctor for more help and he prescribed several things.

I would say, more than any other physical response, sleeping helped. Grief is exhausting and sleep gives you a break both physically and mentally to do it all again the next day. If you are struggling to sleep, seek help from a professional. Prescription medication isn't for everyone and I was hesitant, but I couldn't have survived without it. There is no healing, no logical thought, no strength, no way to survive the pain if you aren't getting enough sleep.

Just know that we all have a variety of physical responses to emotional pain and grief. I had some extreme reactions. It's important to monitor those responses so they don't add to your psychological and emotional pain. It is nearly impossible to take care of yourself physically when you are dealing with this much emotional pain. If possible, give this responsibility to someone else. People want to help but don't know what to do. I had a family and friends who would just say, "Take a drink... let's go get a massage... let's go for a walk... take a vitamin... take your meds." Once I gave this responsibility to someone else, I began to physically heal a little.

Cast all your anxiety on him because he cares for you.

———————

1 Peter 5:7

October 25, 2014

Stress is one of those forces that you know is not good for you, however, you don't have the ability to stop or control it. It affects you i so many ways. It damages and changes your body, mind, soul, spirit, faith, hope, expectations and your outlook in general.

My stress all stems from Larry and Sandra's death which has created an overwhelming sense of my own mortality and loneliness. When the two people you cherish and love more than yourself are suddenly ripped from your life, the stress from grief overcomes you like a tsunami hitting the isle that lays in its path.

For me, stress has hit my body. Just 2 months and 9 days after the accidents, I've lost 20 lbs, I cant sleep, I have a constant headache, and a constant burning in every muscle of my body. I can't escape it no matter how hard I try. My stomach produces so much acids that I have constant issues. I can't keep up. I feel as if I'm sometimes losing the battle.

Stress also manifest itself

The LORD is faithful to all His promises and loving toward all He has made.
Psalm 145:13

in the form of anxiety. Both mild and constant as well as sudden acute attacks. My hands constantly shake and I can't, no matter how hard I try, make them stop. It is if every ounce of stress and grief is fighting my body to be released. At times the grief overwhelms me and the panic attack is sudden and intense. I find it hard to breathe and it feels as if the weight of everything is sitting on my chest trying to stifle every breath until it's my last. In addition, I can't focus. I find it hard to think about

In You, O Lord, do I put my trust and confidently take refuge;
let me never be put to shame or confusion!
Psalm 71:1

anything except Larry, Landon and the accident for more than a few moments at a time. No matter how much I try, my mind continually takes me back to that phone call and the accident.

I feel everything else in life is completely unworthy of energy, thought, and concentration. How can anything else be of significance? I hear others talking about the lives, circumstances, families and stress. I want to scream. How can they complain about their spouse and children? How can they be so ungrateful for the very thing I've

lost and can no longer
have and hold?

Stress has challenged my
faith. I used to think that
I was a praying woman
and that I knew God. I've
since learned different. My
relationship with Christ is
one of complete dependence. I
feel his comfort and presence.
I know I'm only surviving
because of His Grace. I
find myself in constant prayer
asking for help to cope,
understand, grieve, stop
grieving, think, handle
situations and just get out
of bed.

At times I feel like I will survive.
Other days I feel as if the stress and
weight is just pushing me under.

Depend on the Lord in whatever you do,
and your plans will succeed.
Proverbs 16:3

06
Chapter

Dreams

Sometimes the mind can create images that haunt us. This was especially true regarding the crash. The first two nights after hearing Landon and Larry had been killed, I had the most awful dreams. I dreamt of the crash, Larry panicking, Landon crying, the explosion, the fire. It was awful. I was consumed with images that haunted me. These were not images I had seen; they were images created in my mind as I had not looked at any images on the news or on social media. Yet my mind painted awful, vivid, gruesome images in my head. I knew that the nightmares could really mess me up if I let them.

In my mind, I understood enough to know that satan was at the root of these. I remembered, all throughout the Bible God used dreams in powerful ways as prophecy, as warnings, and even as hints of His glory, but, these were not those kinds of dreams. These were nightmares that were meant to bring fear, to drive out peace, to cause anger, and to destroy. I prayed:

For God hath not given us the spirit of fear; but of power, and of love and of sound mind.

---

2 Timothy 1:7

I told God I knew I couldn't survive if the nightmares continued. I asked God to drive satan out and remove the horrible images. I quoted scripture and prayed 2 Timothy 1:7 every time I had an image creep into my head.

Thankfully, God immediately healed my mind of those nightmares. Not once since saying and repeating that prayer have I been plagued by nightmares. God has been faithful to this. I remained faithful in making sure I ended each day reading scripture and asking God for peaceful sleep.

If you are struggling with nightmares, God can heal and help you too. Fill your mind with the things you want to dwell on. Read devotions of hope, peace, and love. Pray often and ask God to drive out satan. I believe God will honor that request and protect your mind from the horrors.

Later, for a long time, I didn't dream at all or at least I don't remember dreaming at all. I remember wanting to see Landon and Larry in my dreams. Finally, God allowed me to dream or has Himself come to me through some unique dreams. It was about three weeks after the accident and I hadn't had any dreams since the nightmares of the first few nights. One night Larry came to me in a dream. We were sitting on a bench. The space was empty and all white. He told me he was sorry. I asked what had happened. He told me the left engine had stalled and failed. I asked if he knew the plane was going to crash. He said, "Yes, at some point, when the engine had stalled and the plane began to fall..." I asked if Landon was scared or if he knew what was happening. Larry answered that he didn't think so because he was tired and was sleeping in the back seat.

About six weeks later, an attorney told me that the NTSB had determined that the left engine had failed. Is it a coincidence? Was it just a dream? Was it a message from God? I believe it was a message from God and that He used the image of Larry to comfort me and give me peace.

For the longest time I didn't or couldn't dream of Landon. I would pay that God would send me images, but they just didn't appear. However, my nephew who was the same age as Landon was dreaming a lot. As a 10-year-old, his dreams were typical child's play. He would dream of him and Landon playing baseball, playing on the playground, swimming in the pool, etc. He was having a hard time with losing his cousin and uncle; children often don't fully understand why their best friend is gone. My sister shared with me that her son had been dreaming a lot. One day she called and said she wanted to share a special dream. Her son had walked in that morning and told her he had a dream about Landon but it was different. Here is an account of his dream:

"I saw Landon last night. We were in a white room. Landon and I talked a lot but his mouth didn't move. He talked to me through our minds. He told me not to worry, that he was with Jesus. We could just hear each other. We talked for a long time and then he said he had to go. The whole time I couldn't see Landon's face but I knew it was him. Finally, I asked him why I couldn't see his face. He told me it was because he had just been with Jesus."

I was blown away by this story. My young nephew had been raised in church, however, he was young, just turned 10. He had heard stories, and of course could tell you stories, however, there is much he didn't understand. My sister and I recalled that in the Bible God appeared to Moses in a burning bush but Moses hid his face and was unable to look upon the Holy Face of God. I'm not sure what all happened in my nephew's dream but I feel certain of this. My child had been with his Heavenly Father, and maybe because he had been in the presence of Jesus, he could not show his face to my nephew. God has some mysterious ways of showing up. From that moment on, my nephew began to heal. He felt the presence of his Heavenly Father come to him in a unique way and God gave him a peace that passed all understanding.

It was several years later, but I finally had this dream about Landon: I was in a large field. The field had a square marked off on it about the size of a football field. Landon and other children were playing inside of the square marking. I was on the outside of it. He ran up to me. We hugged. I told him how much I loved and missed him. He told me Heaven was perfect and that Jesus took care of him. He told me everything was ok and that I couldn't stay. He told me he loved me and would see me soon.

Again, I believe God sent Landon's image to me to give me peace. I haven't dreamed of either Larry or Land much since then, but when I do it's always one of them assuring me that everything is ok. I know, without a doubt, that God has protected my mind from all the nightmares and has sent dreams and images to assure me and to give me peace.

Each of us had a dream the same night, and each dream had a meaning of its own.

Genesis 41:11

"We both had dreams", they answered, "but there is no one to interpret them." Then Joseph said to them, "Do not interpretations belong to God? Tell me your dreams."

Genesis 40:8

October 16, 2014

Today was a tough day
as most are. I heard from
the litigation attorney today.
He thinks there is a good
case against several.

Two weeks after the accident,
I was back at home. I had
not had any dreams since the
nightmares of the first night
I had been asking God to
let me dream of them. One
night (sometime after Labor day)
I had that dream. Larry
came to me. We were sitting
on a bench. He told me he was
sorry. I asked what had
happened. He told me the
left engine failed. I asked

if he knew he was going to die. He said yes; as soon as the plane began to nose dive. I asked if Landon knew. He said he didn't know but he didn't think so since Landon wasn't feeling well and was laying down in the back.

 Today the attorney tells me that they had determined that the left engine had failed.

I is it coincidence. Was it a dream. Is it from God. I believe the dream was from him. Maybe he sent Larry. Maybe he sent the dream. I believe its real. Todays attorney affirmed something for me.

07
Chapter

"Please, Just Help Me"

As you can imagine, I was an emotional mess after the accident. My family insisted I start counseling right away. As a counselor myself, I knew the importance of therapy, however, I wasn't sure I was ready to start talking about all of this. I knew I wanted to see someone who had also lost a child. It was important to me that someone could really empathize with the loss of a child. I knew exactly who to contact. Dr. Darlene Hunter had been a college professor previously and she too had lost a child. I knew she could refer me in the right direction. I called her and she graciously offered to start seeing me herself. She also reminded me she had lost a spouse, as well, and she was a Christian; I knew she would give me sound, scriptural advice.

I remember that first counseling session so vividly. I kept dreading it. I spent hours the day before just thinking about how that session would go. *What would I say? How could I talk about it? How could I talk about them? What would happen if I just couldn't speak? How could she help me? How could I ever heal? How do I do this?*

My mother drove me to that first session, as I was still not staying alone and couldn't focus enough to drive a car. I sat quietly on the drive over and contemplated all those questions again. As my mother pulled up to the door, I remember saying, "I'm not sure I'm ready for this." She said, "I know, but you have to." I slowly walked to the door and knocked. The moment I saw Dr. Hunter, I fell apart and fell into her arms in the doorway, "Please just help me," I sobbed. She held me in that moment and told me we would do it together.

Therapy was good but hard. I cried a lot. I went every day for about two weeks, then I backed off and went twice a week. After about a month I settled into seeing Dr. Hunter once a week and that lasted for about six months. In the beginning, I just sobbed, "I can't do this; I don't want to do this." It was all I could think. I just wanted to hold them again.

Dr. Hunter was so patient and helped me move beyond the paralysis of it all. She helped me move to acceptance and then stayed with me through all the stages of grief and ranges of emotions. We talked about everything from wanting to die to dating. It was good to have someone outside of family and friends who wouldn't judge those feelings. She helped me to understand, to process my emotions and stress. She suggested I see a doctor about regulating my medication and recommended yoga.

Why is counseling so important during grief? Throughout grief, we experience a wide range of emotions including sadness, denial, loneliness, anger, guilt, shame, helplessness, emptiness, fear, hopelessness, yearning, guilt, and desperation. It's difficult to process just one of those alone and nearly impossible to process them all at once as they fly at you unexpectedly and come at you like tsunamis. Counseling/therapy will help you accept the reality of the loss, work through the pain, and then adjust to a new life without your loved ones.

I also attended group grief counseling through my church. The coming together of individuals who were also grieving was both overwhelming at times and yet very healing. That group of people helped me to know that what I was feeling was normal. They also constantly cried. We processed together, listened to each other, and had empathy that only another grieving soul would understand. It was comforting to know I was not alone in my feelings.

Regardless of what form of counseling you decide to use, just commit. I have been an independent woman my whole life and I have struggled to ask or accept help, but in this instance, I knew I couldn't do it alone. I depended on professionals and groups to support me throughout this process, and this has been key in my healing. Don't hesitate another moment. There is help. There is financial assistance, if needed. No excuses. Just take that step.

For lack of guidance a nation falls, but victory is won through many advisers.

———————

Proverbs 11:14

Plans fail for lack of counsel, but with many advisers they succeed.

———————

Proverbs 15:22

Where there is strife, there is pride, but wisdom is found in those who take advice.

———————

Proverbs 13:10

October 18, 2014

Tonight was grief group. The room was full of people who were hurting and in pain who had lost loved ones. I remember Ann, an 82 year old woman who lost her husband of 51 years. She was so heartbroken. Tonight we watched a video about grief. After we held hands and went around the room to say the names of the people we loved and lost.

"My husband Larry of 20 years and my 9 year old son Landon just 2 months ago."

The word of the LORD is right and true;
He is faithful in all He does.

Psalm 33:4

71

It was so hard just to say their names out loud and verbalize the loss. Grief overwhelmed me and I lost all control.

My heart is so broken. How can this be real? How can it be happening? God, why me? Why them? Why both? This hurts too bad. Please take me. Please let me die. Please let me see them soon. I miss them so much. This is just so hard. I proclaim your peace, comfort, & strength. I cannot do this Jesus. Please carry me through this valley of shadow of death.

The LORD is my strength, my shield from every danger.
I trust in Him with all my heart.
Psalm 28:7

08
Chapter

Get Her Some Medicine

I don't claim to be a doctor, nor do I want to give you any medical advice. I simply strive to share my experience with medications here. First, it's important to know that my own personality is such that I've never been a huge fan of medications and chemicals in general. I am a firm believer that God gave us everything we need to naturally heal our bodies through the earth. Yet, I ended up taking medicine. I don't say this lightly, but medicine does have its place and you shouldn't hesitate to ask for help if you need it.

Within hours of the accident, in those moments of uncontrollable crying, I could hear people talking about this: "Just call a doctor and get her some medicine," I heard one friend tell another. That conversation was repeated several times. Again, when my sisters arrived, I could hear again,

"Just get her some medicine." Within a couple days of losing Larry and Landon, my sisters took me to a doctor's office. This was not my doctor, nor had I ever seen this doctor before. The doctor assessed me for suicide and prescribed an anti-depressant and something to help me sleep. In those early days, I needed them just to function. I couldn't sleep. All I did was cry. With the medicine, I was able to get enough sleep, 4-6 hours a night, and at least function. The feeling of the weight on my chest was just constant anxiety. The medicine helped me feel like I could breathe. It certainly numbed me, but in those first few weeks, I needed it. I knew deep down that I didn't want to stay on meds long term or for the rest of my life, but I also knew enough to understand how much I needed them at that point.

About two weeks later, when I was back at home, I went to see my family physician who had treated me for the past 20 years. I sat in the examination room waiting for him to arrive. I told myself I would tell him about the accident, tell him I wanted to get off the medicine, ask for something to sleep, and be out of there. I heard the tap on the door. Dr. Andrew Metzr walked in, looked at me and said, "Hello. Good to see you. What's going on?" Then it happened, in one breath my whole plan went down the drain. I opened my mouth to speak, the sobbing started and then I hyperventilated. When I could breathe again, and in between sobs, I told him about the plane crash, losing Larry and Landon, and about the last couple of weeks. He sat beside me with his arms wrapped around me, telling me how sorry he was. I mentioned getting off the anti-depressants and anti-anxiety medicine and he hugged me as he said, "It's just not time. It's just too early." At that moment, I knew he was right. I wasn't functioning. I was a mess and I needed medical help.

He knew my ultimate wishes to be off medicine, but he also advised me against getting off meds at that time. He worked with me to ensure I was in therapy, sleeping, getting exercise, finding ways to relax, and to set goals. We talked about a plan to begin to decrease meds after the holidays, in about five months.

He worked hard to help me find the right combinations. One drug left me with a terrible metal taste in my mouth, one made me gain weight, one made me so tired I couldn't function, one made me have vivid dreams that Larry and Landon really weren't dead. As you can imagine, that was the worst side effect of all. Most important, I stuck with it and I eventually found a combination that worked. I was on an antidepressant, an anti-anxiety med, as needed, and a sleep aid, as needed, combined with natural sleep aids on a regular basis. I stayed on this combination through Landon's birthday, Thanks-giving, Christmas, New Year's and then started a plan to come off my medications in January.

The doctor slowly began to reduce the meds, keeping in constant communication about my mental state along the way. By March I was off all medications and on herbal supplements, however, in June, as Larry's birthday, our anniversary, and the August anniversary of their deaths begin to approach, I was struggling to hold on. I was crying all the time. I found myself struggling to sleep, eat, exercise, and to have positive thoughts. I called my doctor and made an appointment. As soon as I saw him, I burst into tears. I couldn't stop crying and then the hyper-ventilating started. "I can't do this," I cried. He quickly sat beside me, wrapped his arms around me as he had at our earlier visit, and told me he was there to help. He suggested I get back on a low dose antidepressant and keep a stronger anti-anxiety available when those attacks came. Slowly but surely, the intense depression began to lift, and I began to function again. To be honest, that pattern persisted a few times over the next several years. My doctor was patient and walked with me every step of that journey.

Admittedly, medicine has its place. Do not hesitate to get the meds you need. Being able to function, breathe, think, eat, and sleep is necessary to move through and process grief. Work closely with a trusted physician, preferably one who knows you well. Let him or her know your goals. My doctor often reminded me that if I needed meds for an ear infection, I wouldn't hesitate to take them. If needed medication for a physical condition, I wouldn't hesitate to take them for the rest of my life. This was great reasoning and I'm glad I listened.

Now, many years later, I'm on a healthy dose of herbal supplements that help me maintain good emotional and mental health. Again, I worked with my physician to find what worked for me. If there is any advice I would give, it would be to seek help when needed and always consult a healthcare provider.

He heals the brokenhearted, binding up their wounds.

Psalms 147:3

09
Chapter

The Dark Place

What I know is that the deeper the love, the deeper the grief. I loved deeply. My husband of 19 1/2 years was more than a spouse, he was my best friend. We had been married for 10 years before we decided to have a child. We were true companions. We really complimented each other and enjoyed our time together. We were both divorced and came from broken marriages, so we had an appreciation for the friendship we had developed. We cherished our time together and made the most of every moment.

Those first five years we were married we lived on a boat in a marina in Clear Lake. What fun times. I was teaching at the time, and we would spend the three summer months taking our boat on some of the most amazing adventures. We would often skip school and work and have a day playing on the lake. We would jet ski, water ski, sunbathe and splash in the water. We would anchor out in coves all around Clear Lake and Galveston Bay. We would cook hamburgers and hot dogs on the grill on the back of our boat and life often felt like one big picnic. One of our favorite things to do was sit on our swim platform with our feet dangling in the water. We would spend hours there just talking and snacking on rice crispy treats. We even took long boat vacations to Destin, Florida via the Intercoastal Waterway. What beautiful memories I have of all those adventures.

About 10 years into our marriage, we were blessed with Landon. He was Larry's third child, but only boy. He had two girls from his first marriage. However, Landon was my only child. I fell in love with him the instant I learned of him. That love grew even more the moment I held him. I never could have imagined I could love anyone more than I loved Larry. It was truly the first time I experienced unconditional love. I would sneak into his room at night and get him out of his crib and hold him, rock him, and sing to him. I loved watching him sleep. He was absolutely perfect.

After having Landon, we purchased a sailboat and named her Sea Dawn; it was a play on my name Charlotte Dawn. We would spend every weekend together on that boat. We would often take off on adventures. We also had an airplane, so on longer breaks we would travel around the Caribbean, dreaming of the days we could live full-time sailing around and island hopping or living on an island. Life was perfect with perfect future plans until that dreadful phone call.

Not only did I lose the two most important people in my life that day, but I also lost all hope. Not only were they my life, but they also were my future. I didn't know how to exist without the two of them. Grief began to take me to some dark places.

The therapist I was seeing asked often about suicidal thoughts. In the beginning, the thoughts weren't suicidal. True, I wished I were dead, I wished I could go to Heaven with Larry and Landon, I wished I weren't in pain, but I wasn't suicidal, but slowly I drifted further and further into the darkness. At this point, early on, I still had people staying around the clock with me. A different friend came and spent every night with me. A different family member or two would come every weekend from Fort Worth to Manvel and stay the weekend. About four weeks after the accident, I decided to go back to work. I just couldn't sit at home every day and do nothing but think about how much I missed them. Work helped. Running a large 6A high school demanded a lot and it kept my mind occupied. It was a welcomed distraction from the pain.

At the realization that my life was forever changed and I would be without Larry and Landon set in, the darkness began to creep back in. I began to sleep a lot, partly because I was depressed and sleep was a break from the pain, and partly because grief and constant crying were so exhausting. In the early months and with the help of medicine, I would sleep 12-16 hours a night and was often still exhausted. The thoughts began to change from wishing I were dead; I did begin thinking about taking my own life.

The pain and grief began to be more than I could bear at times. It was the end of October and I decided I was sending everyone home. One evening, I sat down and wrote an email to all of them and told them it was time for me to start taking charge of my own life and staying alone. I told them all how much I appreciated all they had done but that I was stronger and could handle this. Halloween night would be the last night anyone would stay with me. I would begin life alone November 1.

My son's 10th birthday was approaching on November 18th, and I couldn't bear the thought of surviving his birthday without him. The doctors had prescribed plenty of medicine and with changing prescriptions I had quite the stockpile of narcotics that would do the job. I had picked a night the week before Landon's birthday. I would simply go home from work on a Friday, take all the meds, go to sleep, and never wake again. I had decided to take my own life. But God had other plans, that day He sent an angel to intervene.

For whatever reason, I had to make a trip to the school district central office that day. While walking past one of the offices, a dear friend, Stephanie Lirette, called me in. She told me that she had been meaning to reach out and when she saw me walk by it was the perfect time. She recalled the story of losing her son and how hard the journey had been. She told me I could walk this journey with God or without Him; it would be easier if I ran to Him and walked beside my Heavenly Father. That day, she reminded me that God created us as eternal beings. God created me to always be a mom. She went on to say that my son was just living in

Heaven with his Heavenly Father, and I needed to live a life that would make him proud of his mom.

Wow, those words struck a chord deep within me. I wanted nothing more than to make my son proud. I adored him. He was the best gift I ever received and the best part of me. I knew I couldn't take my own life and make him proud. That day, I decided not only to survive, but also to live and thrive. I would do everything possible to make sure my story helped just one other person.

I later shared this story with Stephanie. She had no idea and didn't even remember the details of the conversation. She simply stepped out and followed God, or her gut, or whatever you want to call it, and spoke to a friend. I will forever be grateful to Stephanie for saving my life that day.

I later got a tattoo. It is a heart that says "love" and has a semicolon in the middle. The semicolon is the symbol of suicide prevention and hope. You see, when you want to end a sentence you put a period. However, if the sentence just must continue with something more to say, you add a semicolon and continue with the message. My life didn't end that day; my story goes on.

If you are in that place, there is HOPE. This life is not the end. We get to spend eternity with those we love, if we choose to have faith in God. If you find yourself feeling helpless and hopeless, just reach out to one individual and ask for help. If you know someone who could be struggling, don't hesitate to ask questions, encourage, check, and ensure safety.

Do not be anxious about anything, but in every situation, by prayer and petition, with thanksgiving, present your requests to God. And the peace of God, which transcends all understanding, will guard your hearts and your minds in Christ Jesus.

Philippians 4:6-7

Cast all your anxiety on him because he cares for you.

---

1 Peter 5:7

I have told you these things, so that in me you may have peace. In this world you will have troubles, But take heart! I have overcome the world.

John 16:33

Peace I leave with you; my peace I give you. I do not give to you as the world gives. Do not let your hearts be troubled and do not be afraid.

John 14:27

Blessed are the peacemakers, for they will be called the children of God.

Matthew 5:9

November 2, 2014

There is an idea that this tragedy can somehow bring glory to God. I don't know how. I really hope that some good can come of this. I know I have to trust God and assume that there is a bigger picture that my life somehow fits into. It all still seems so unreal. I'm not at a place yet where I can give God glory & praise for this, but I can give him glory and praise for the good he has brought into my life. I can thank him for the family and friends

My soul finds rest in God alone; my salvation comes from Him.
Psalm 62:1

and support and love.
Its hard to see good but
I know its there.
I miss my family.
The emptiness and loneliness
is too much. I just want
to be with them. I want
to see them again. I can't
imagine waiting a lifetime.
I can't imagine my whole
life without them. Its
just too hard. I love you
and miss you both.

10
Chapter

Surviving Holidays and Celebrations

Landon's birthday

Landon's birthday is November 18th. That first birthday without him was just three months after the day they died. As time went by, that day was looming like an ominous storm just off in the distance. It was dark and gray. I could hear and see it approaching and my chest felt heavy with its impending arrival. The lightning flashes slowly came closer, and with each day the rolling thunder grew louder and louder. That storm threatened to devastate my already broken heart and shake my existence even more. With complete dread, I kept questioning, *How do I celebrate my son's birth, when his life has been ripped from my grasp?*

All I can say is, I'm thankful for friends and family. They kept asking what I wanted to do. I didn't know; I couldn't answer. During the first few days after the accident, I had developed a memorial scholarship fund in Landon's name and had requested donations in lieu of flowers. My husband and son loved Chick-Fil-A™. It was their go-to meal and every Saturday morning breakfast. My friend contacted our local franchise. Within minutes we had a celebration location, and to my surprise, a portion of the profits that evening would be donated to Landon's scholarship fund.

How did I survive that first birthday celebration?

First, I had to come to the realization that I cherished those nine precious years more than anything I had ever experienced. I would rather have had those nine years and lost Landon, than to have never had them at all. I had to also remember to thank God regularly for those nine years and for allowing me to be so blessed as Landon's mom. I began to understand that a mom's intense pain after her loss of a child was a direct reflection of her intense love. I wanted to own that love and therefore I had to own the pain. I didn't quite know how to do that, and still don't have it all figured out, but that will come.

Second, I had to completely relinquish control and let someone else handle everything. As a mom, my heart was completely consumed. I couldn't think clearly, much less organize a plan. My best friend, Leslie, has great discernment and a heart for me and my pain. She understood that it was all too painful, and yet I needed to know that my son was being honored. I know that having someone I trusted take control allowed me to sit back and focus on emotionally surviving the day while honoring my precious son was key to the success of that first birthday.

Finally, I had no expectations of myself or anyone else. This seems almost silly but was key. I had to walk into that day with absolutely no expectations. I could not place the weight of that day on expectations of what others might or might not do. I had to put my trust in God to help me honor my son, celebrate, remember those nine precious years, and give God the glory, no matter what.

Well, the evening was a huge success. I couldn't tell you what we raised for the scholarship fund, and it doesn't matter. That night, hundreds of family and friends stopped by to honor Landon and share in one of his favorite meals. We all laughed together (this was the first time I laughed since the accident), cried together, told stories, and held each other close that night. I remember so many of his friends and their families stopping by and sharing their stories of how they celebrated Landon's birthday. The communities of Manvel, Pearland, and Alvin come to support us in a way I could never have imagined. It truly was a celebration of Landon's birth and his life.

Now, I celebrate a little differently. Each year I still eat Chick-Fil-A™, however, there are no big gatherings or parties. I encourage people all over the community, state, nation, and world to join me in eating Chick-Fil-A™ and sharing their pictures on social media. It's this mom's greatest joy to remember her precious son and to know that others remember him too. No matter how you choose to celebrate, remembering or honoring is up to you. Don't let others dictate that for you. You and your loved ones must decide what works for you. However, you do it, just make sure to stop, be still, remember, and give honor. Although painful, there is great healing in these moments.

For loved ones who live with someone who has lost a child, navigating this day can be difficult. Here are some things that may help.

- Acknowledge the day. Someone once told me they thought about me on Landon's birthday but didn't want to say anything because they were afraid to make me sad. This thoughtful person just had no idea. Those of us who have lost loved ones, especially children, think of them hundreds of times a day. We are acutely aware their birthday is approaching or is here. Although it feels uncomfortable, acknowledging the day will go a long way to show your loved one your empathy. If you just don't know what to say, a card is a perfect way to acknowledge the day.

- Don't plan this day for your loved one who is still grieving. Instead, ask them what they want to do? My sister, who loves me dearly, wanted to plan a big celebration for Landon's birthday that second year. I just couldn't do it. I'm glad she asked; I was able to say no but I appreciated the offer. Instead, I had a quiet dinner with a friend at one of Landon's favorite places.

- Be patient and give a lot of grace. For me, this day is filled with a roller coaster of emotions, and on top of that, every emotion is magnified. Remember, nothing that happens on that day is about you. It's really about a lot of grief and surviving one of the toughest days of the year.

November 18, 2014

Today Landon turns 10. My time with him was so precious but too short. I miss him so much. I remember the day he was born. I was instantly in love. I couldn't get enough of him. I would pick up from his crib when he slept and hold and kiss him. I remember the way he would say "Mom, I love you". He really did love his mom. We used to say we were in love with each other and we were. It was the best love I ever experienced. I tried to celebrate and honor

In You, O Lord, do I put my trust and confidently take refuge;
let me never be put to shame or confusion!
Psalm 71:1

him on this 10th birthday. I tried to be thankful for the best 10 years of my life. I tried to heal. I miss him so terribly much. I long to hold him in my arms and kiss his beautiful face. I long to tell him how much I love him. I have to believe in the promises of heaven, eternity, joy, and seeing my Landon again. I choose to believe and have faith in God's word. Anything else would be too unbearable. I know I'll spend eternity with my precious child.

"Be strong and courageous. The LORD your God will be
with you wherever you go."
Joshua 1:9

My wedding anniversary

The loss of Larry was not just the loss of my spouse, he truly was my best friend. Because of the unique circumstance of my losing both my husband and child, at first, I couldn't grieve Larry. I know that sounds strange, but my love and the pain of losing my child was so overwhelming that I just couldn't. When I did, it was different.

I grieved my soulmate. I grieved having someone to talk to, having a warm body next to me, intimacy, and my best friend. When I was finally able to start grieving the loss of my husband, it was as if I started all over again. It really hit me hard that second anniversary without him.

I choose to celebrate our anniversary differently than I do other holidays and birthdays. It's personal, it's quiet, it's just me. I spend time each year trying to remember some of the best times of our marriage. I recollect about trips, anniversary gifts, fun experiences, laughing together and so much more. I thank God for that type of love and ask Him to provide it again. I often watch a movie we enjoyed together, I fix some of our favorite foods, I often cry, but I always cherish the sweet memories.

November 1, 2014

Larry,

I can't believe its been two and a half months since the accident. I wish I had gone with you that day. More, I wish I had never bought you flying lessons 20 years ago, or allowed you to buy a plane or to take Landon. I miss you so much. I miss your friendship and companionship and talking to you each night. The house feels so empty. My heart feels so empty. I miss your warm touch and our intimate times together. I'm so lonely I can't imagine ever loving another man. You were my soul mate and my best friend.

I trust in Your unfailing love. I will rejoice because You have rescued me.
I will sing to the LORD because He has been so good to me.
Psalm 13:5-6

Watch over my Landon. I know he is good. I'm glad he has you. I know he's happy but I miss him so much. Please tell him I love him and wrap your arms tightly around him and tell him they are ~~big~~ hugs from his mama. I love you. I miss you so much.

Love, Charlotte.

Thanksgiving

Thanksgiving? How can I give thanks? The shock has long worn off from that dreadful day in August. As a family, Larry, Landon, and I celebrated most Thanksgivings on vacation somewhere special. Some years were spent at Disney World, riding rides; we spent many in the Bahamas, laying on a beach, while others were in the mountains skiing and snowmobiling. We had just moved to our new house the weekend before Thanksgiving 2013. For the first time, we had family in our new home. What a blessing that turned out to be. I will forever treasure that last Thanksgiving with Larry and Landon.

As that first Thanksgiving after the accident approached, the dread consumed me. We had already booked and planned a trip to Las Vegas for Thanksgiving 2014. I knew I couldn't go without them. It just didn't seem right, but I was so consumed with grief I couldn't bring myself to cancel the plans, much less make new plans.

There is no sugar-coating things; that first Thanksgiving after Larry and Landon died was awful. All my family lived in the Dallas/Ft. Worth area. I was off work all week, so my sister drove to Manvel to pick me up and take me back home with her to spend that first Thanksgiving. I have a huge family. I am one of five girls and there are many nieces and nephews. Extended family time was generally chaotic, but comforting. That first Thanksgiving, though, was different. It was excruciating, overwhelming and downright agonizing; "painful" often comes to mind. My emotions were completely raw, and I was still crying all day, every day.

Thanksgiving at my family's house was just as it had been every other year, chaotic. Except this time, there was a hole. Families and children were everywhere, and it was a heartbreaking reminder of the stark reality that my whole family was gone. Images haunted me. I could almost see my Larry's face as he would have been playing pool and watching football with the brothers-in-law. The faint laughter of my son, Landon, echoed in my head and heart as children ran through the house. Family kept finding me hiding somewhere, crying, trying to get through this laboriously painful day. I had not at all prepared for this.

Looking back, I would have done it all differently, but I learned a lot that first Thanksgiving. I had to redefine what Thanksgiving really meant, how I would be thankful and celebrate for years to come, and finally how I would give thanks to God.

As I prepare for Thanksgiving now, I often remember Philippians 4:6: *"Do not be anxious about anything, but in every situation, by prayer and petition, with thanksgiving, present your requests to God."* How can I not be anxious and in everything be thankful? At first, this verse made me angry. Over and over, I cried to God, "I will not be thankful for this." It took me a long time and significant time in prayer and Bible study to realize that this was NOT what God was asking me to do. God was asking me to be thankful for the time and blessing that I did have and cherish every memory.

Charlotte Liptack

I thank my God every time I remember you.

Philippians 1:3.

God was asking me to trust His plan. I don't yet know God's plan for my life, however, I trust.

Trust in the Lord with all your heart and lean not on your own understanding.

Proverbs 3:5.

God was asking me to remember to give Him glory.

I will praise God's name in song and glorify him with thanksgiving.

Psalm 69:30.

This was tough. I read David's psalm, I read Job's journey, I read Joseph's story. All of these warriors for Christ doubted, questioned and even asked, "Why?" Through each story I learned how to trust that God's plan was bigger than my journey, my life, my pain, and my suffering. Each reminded me that this life was about bringing people to Jesus so that they could love with the same HOPE and know that one day they would spend eternity with their loved ones at the feet of Jesus. They reminded me to be thankful for HOPE.

We have this HOPE as an anchor for the soul, firm and secure.

Hebrews 6:19.

Now, I spend Thanks-giving much differently than I did that first year. I start that day with a list of the things for which I am thankful.

- More than 20 years with my amazing husband Larry who loved and adored me

- Nine years as Mom to the most amazing little soul I will ever know

- That I got to pray with my son the previous Easter as he asked Jesus to be his Savior

- I will spend eternity in Heaven

- That God has used my story to help others on their journey

The list goes on and one but you get the picture. I must be literal and intentional with this practice. I write it down and share it with others every year. I cannot urge you enough to do the same. It keeps my life, my loss, my eternity in perspective.

December 1, 2014

Thanksgiving was hard.
I thought about them
several times throughout
the day. It was so sad
to see Braden so lonely
with noone to play with.
Everyone had someone
but me. It felt horrible
and lonely. I know I
have so much to be
thankful for.
1) Faith & relationship w/ God
2) family (parents & sisters)
3) friends
4) Lauren & Gul
5) memories
6) work
7) home

The LORD is my rock, my fortress and my deliverer;
my God is my rock, in whom I take refuge.
Psalm 18:2

8) Church
9) I'm taken care of

I would give most of it up to have my family back. I still find myself trying to wrap me head around this. Today I cleaned out Larrys closets and drawers. It was hard but it helps me move forward. I didn't want to do it because I was afraid of what he would say if he returned. Sounds crazy I know. Thats why I had to do it. I had to ack nowledge that they aren't coming back. The Thanksgiving week made me realize I don't want to do Christmas. I just can't go do all of that stuff. I need to do something different and remember Christ! I need to remember how he gave his son for me, Larry and Landon.

I want to stay busy these next three weeks yet focus enough to make good plans.

I've emailed Ron & Mary about Panama.

I pray football team does well and goes to State & wins. I need something good and positive to look forward to.

The word of the LORD is right and true;
He is faithful in all He does.
Psalm 33:4

Christmas

The tough things about loss are the constant reminders of what you once had. Christmas only magnifies it all. As I look back at my journals over the years, the journals around the holiday are filled with tear-stained pages that are riddled with pain.

Dec 28, 2014 - (The first Christmas after my husband and son died.) Christmas was nearly unbearable. How do you celebrate the Christmas holidays when you've lost your best friend and only child? I'm trying so hard to stay focused on Christ. I know Christ is enough but I'm drowning. They are supposed to be here! Larry and I are supposed to grow old together watching our Landon grow his own family. Now what?

December 14, 2015 - Tomorrow marks two weeks until Christmas. It feels like I can hardly breathe. I can't bear the thought of Christmas without the two best gifts I ever received. Holidays symbolize love, family, togetherness, traditions and memories. This Christmas is an acute reminder of what I no longer have. It feels like a slap in the face. It's as if Christmas is saying, "You lost your husband and child, you have no family, there are no traditions, you are alone." How do I find the strength to put all those negative thoughts aside? How do I survive this time of year?

December 18, 2016 - This year, I will try and do Christmas. In a small way. It must be different. I can't bear the same traditions without Larry and Landon. I'm going with a friend to Alabama. I'm not sure if I want to go; not sure I want to spend the holidays with him. If I do go, no one will understand my pain, my loss, my grief, the struggle, much less the overwhelming anxiety. Does this ever get easier? Can I ever again enjoy the holidays?

December 10th, 2017 - How do I celebrate Christmas? How do I enjoy the holidays? How do I survive another year? Why, God Why? I don't know if I have the answers to any of these questions. For my family, Christmas has always been a celebration of God's ultimate sacrifice and Christ's birth. However, like most of you, it was also about creating family memories and spoiling my son. Like many of you, my/our Christmas was grounded in traditions; some from our own childhoods, some new that we created as a family. Now what?

As that first Christmas approached, I didn't know what to do, how to do it, who to spend it with, and how to continue to celebrate. That first Christmas came so quickly after the accident. I had just survived my son's first birthday since his death and the first Thanksgiving after loss. I tried Christmas shopping one day. After breaking down into hysterical sobs and running out of the store, I knew I had a challenging month ahead. I knew it was important for my family to spend some time with me and to know I was ok, yet I knew I couldn't endure the traditional Christmas celebration. That year I felt so alone, yet I was surrounded by people. Not a lot has changed in that regard. It was as if I was in the middle of the ocean in the apex of the storm. Just as I was able to get my head above water, another wave would crash, pushing me under. I was fighting just to breathe, and I was losing. I didn't know how to survive.

That year, I simply ran away. I called some dear friends who had just bought a retirement condo in Panama City, Panama. They invited me down and promised no Christmas tree, no celebration, and no gifts. So I packed a bag and left. Whether it's your first holiday or celebration or your tenth, sometimes you just need to run away. My situation was different in that I had no one else to be responsible for. My only other concern was for my two stepdaughters who would be spending their first Christmas without their brother and dad. However, they were both married. I knew they would be in good hands with their mom and husbands. Not everyone has the option to run away.

Christmas is still unbearable, but I get through. I still can't go Christmas shopping in the stores, so online shopping has become my greatest holiday asset. I still really struggle with Christmas music, Christmas decorations (I don't decorate), Christmas parties, Christmas gift exchanges. I say "no" when I can, however, the rest of the world loves all this, so I endure it for the moment and then go hide and cry.

Regardless of where you are in your journey, you need to think ahead and plan and be prepared for when the waves of grief come crashing down. So how do we survive the holiday season? Here are a few things that have helped me navigate through.

- **Find time to honor your loved one**. Ignoring it isn't an option. You may pretend, but everyone who has ever lost a child, spouse or loved ones knows that their memory consumes your thoughts. It will take someone special to be able to do this with you. It's often too much for many friends and family members. It's not that people don't care, it's that they don't know what to do and lack the coping skills to manage their own feelings about grief, much less support someone else. How you honor your child or loved one will be unique, special, and anchored in the depths of sweet memories. If you have immediate family (spouse and other children) they may want to participate in a new tradition. Do what works for you. Honoring your loved ones can take on many different forms. I had special Christmas ornaments made with their picture; I gave them to everyone. I also had quilts made for my two stepdaughters.

- **Skip the holidays if you need to**. I am single and have no living children so I can and need to do this. Those big family gatherings that I have always been a tradition now cause me a great deal of pain and anxiety. I have a constant lump in my throat, all while fighting back the tears. I have the freedom to skip the holidays, so I do. This year I will be skipping the holidays and scuba diving.

- **Give yourself permission to actively grieve and fall apart**. Because life does go on, it is easy to constantly push our grief down, denying an emotional response. If you don't allow yourself to feel, when you least expect it, it will come out of nowhere and overwhelm you like a sudden deluge. Every year, I remind my family how difficult it is. They know that I will need to step away and cry. They also know my preference is to be alone when I cry. Although difficult, tell others ahead of time what you will and will not need. Explain what you want to do or not do. I assure you that your family may be struggling as well. Having conversations ahead of time will relieve anxiety and give clarity regarding expectations.

- **Allow others to help if it's on your terms.** These are tough days and for those people who are brave enough to reach out, accept the offer. As much as I don't want to engage in huge extended family Thanksgiving and Christmas rituals, I don't want to be alone either. As I said, my first Christmas after losing my husband and son, some dear friends invited me to their condo on the beach in Panama City, Panama. I told them no gifts, no decorations, no Christmas tree. They happily obliged and it was a perfect getaway.

- **Find time to just laugh and breathe.** This sounds so simple but it's harder than it sounds. It's hard to find people to laugh with during the holidays. It's often all so serious, spiritual, and formal, so, I take it upon myself to plan FUN. I try to have an annual girls' happy hour or girls' night. We do nothing but laugh. Then I find time alone and just breathe. It's important to make myself slow down, relax, and to pray and meditate.

- **Remember Jesus** - Finally, focus on the true meaning of Christmas. This is truly the most important thing you can do. Because of Jesus, I have eternal life and so do my loved ones. They have just gone on before me. If you don't know this truth for yourself, reach out. Without Jesus, I could never travel this journey. He is my HOPE. He gives me peace! My hope is grounded in faith. There are times I have to remind myself that God knows the loss of a child. God sent his only Son to one day be crucified for my sins that I may have eternal life. He did this for me, for you, and for any who will accept it.

For those of you who are family and friends of someone who has experienced great loss here are a few helpful hints.

- **This is not about you.** No matter what your loved one does or doesn't do, it's never about you. If they decide to skip the holidays, be gracious; don't take it personally.

- **Offer social opportunities.** Offer opportunities to get together that are different from the traditional holiday experiences. For example, invite a loved one to a movie, go watch a sporting event, go out for dinner and drinks. If they decline, keep asking and remember, IT'S NOT ABOUT YOU.

- **You can't fix this.** You can only offer love, support and understanding. Be patient, offer lots of grace, and pray.

My prayer is that we all find a HOPE and PEACE this holiday season as we remember and celebrate our loved ones.

For unto us a child is born, to us a Son is given.

Isaiah 9:6

For God so loved the world, that he gave his only begotten Son, that whosoever believeth in him should not perish, but have everlasting life. For God sent not his Son into the world to condemn the world; but that the world through him might be saved.

———————

. John 3:16-17

And the peace of God, which transcends all understanding, will guard your hearts and your minds in Christ Jesus.

———————

Philippians 4:7

December 28, 2014

Christmas was nearly unbearable. How in the world do you celebrate Christmas when you've lost your kid and husband. I'm trying so hard to stay focused on Christ. I know Christ is enough but I've been so lonely. I miss Landon so bad I ache. I miss Harry too. Reading the report was horrifying. How do I erase the images? Christmas was hard! There were so many reminders. Being with family was hard. My Harry and Landon are supposed to be here. They

My soul finds rest in God alone; my salvation comes from Him.

Psalm 62:1

111

are supposed to be with me.
We were supposed to grow
old together and support
Landon.

I drove home Christmas
day. I wanted to be
alone. I think I've
cried everyday since
Thanksgiving.

I left the day after for
Panama City, Panama. Its
beautiful and peaceful.
There are no reminders
of Larry and Landon here.
Only the knowing that
they would have loved this
and that this is a vacation
we would have taken
together. I go home
on the 1st. Then what?

Delight yourself in the LORD
and He will give you the desires of your heart.
Psalm 37:4

Now that I have survived these holidays, now what? What do I do now? God, I need you to send me someone. I need to not feel so lonely. I need a person. I need to love. I need a child. I know thats unlikely but please rescue me from this pain, lonliness and emptiness. Help me to find your peace that passes all understanding. I've had peace and I know, its from you. Just please continue to shower me with more of your love, peace, strength. Let 2015 be a true year of new joy & beginnings.

The LORD is my light and my salvation – whom shall I fear?
The LORD is the stronghold of my life – of whom shall I be afraid?
Psalm 27:1

December 29, 2014

Today I sit alone on a balcony in Panama City, Panama. I look out over God's amazing creation: the ocean, the mountains, the rain forest. I wonder why did he take Larry and Landon, two of his most perfect creations. Landon was so innocent. I'm glad he has perfect peace and will never know heartache or loss.

I have so many questions. Some about my loss and why me?, why us? Some questions about heaven. Yet some about future.

The LORD Himself goes before you and will be with you;
He will never leave you nor forsake you.
Deuteronomy 31:8

Questions like...
- When will I get to see them again?
- Will I ever again know happiness like I had w/ Larry & Landon?
- If so when & how?
- What is my purpose? When will you reveal it?
- What is heaven really like?
- Do they know how much I love and miss them?
- Has Landon met his younger brother/sister?
- Do Larry and Landon spend every day together?
- Have they met other children?
- Can they come visit in spirit or dreams?
- Are Pa and Grandma there with them?
- Where is heaven?

God is working in you, giving you the desire
to obey Him and the power to do what pleases Him.
Philippians 2:13

115

As this year draws to a close over these next few days, I want to forget the terror and have only sweet memories. I want to leave the heartache and find perfect peace and comfort. I want to give up loneliness for new joy. I want to draw even closer to God but with a new family. I want to never again take one day, one moment or one opportunity for granted. I want to bask in His perfect presence and light. I want to follow His perfect plan because that is where true joy, peace, and hope lies.

I can do everything through Him who gives me strength.
Philippians 4:13

11
Chapter

God Crossed the Line

I had created an imaginary line in the sand. It really existed only in my mind. I knew that bad things happen all around the world. I knew that bad things could possibly happen in my own extended family. I certainly didn't think they could happen in my personal little circle. I served God, I prayed regularly, my family was faithful, and we did all the right things. That imaginary line, though I never spoke it out loud, went something like this: *"God, I will continue to serve You, I will continue to praise You, I will continue to love You, I will continue to do good. I do all of this and God, You will protect my family, especially Larry and Landon."* It was just how I expected things to work and then one day GOD CROSSED THAT LINE.

I was so angry. How could God allow these awful things to happen? God **crossed the line** when he took my best friend, husband and companion of 19 1/2 years and left me to do life alone. **God crossed the line** when he took the best gift He ever gave me, motherhood. He took my only son and left me feeling like an empty shell. **God crossed the line** when He took everything that mattered to me and left me here to survive this unimaginable nightmare.

So, why do awful things happen to good people? I really don't know. My grief has left me with so many questions and has challenged my faith in so many ways. Losing Larry and Landon rocked my faith to its core. I questioned everything about God's power, His love, and His sovereignty. I couldn't fathom how all three of those things could exist and I could still be suffering such loss.

I truly struggled with God's love. If God really loved me and died for me, why would He allow me to suffer in such unimaginable pain. I began to question if I had caused this suffering. *Did I do something wrong? Is this my condemnation? Is God allowing me to suffer for punishment for choices I had made?* My faith just couldn't reconcile this. I kept desperately searching for answers; I needed to understand. I would lay in bed and cry for hours, "Why God, why?" I searched through God's Word looking for answers. I wanted God to explain this to me. I kept going back to these verses:

Therefore, there is now no condemnation for those who are in Christ Jesus.

Romans 8:1

118

But God demonstrated his own love for us in this: While we were still sinners, Christ died for us.

———————

Romans 5:8

As I began to accept this promise, I heard God's whisper, "This is not about you." That truly infuriated me! *What do you mean this isn't about me? This is completely about me. I am the one without a husband, without a child, struggling to breathe, and struggling to survive. I am the one who feels like an empty shell of a person who is lost and struggling to find myself. This is all about me!*

As I reconciled that this wasn't about my punishment and God's love, I began to question God's power and sovereignty. Sovereignty refers to God's supreme authority and power. I had always been taught that there is absolutely nothing that happens outside of God's influence and authority. He has no limitations. Questioning God's sovereignty meant I was really questioning the foundation of my faith. If God is truly all-powerful, and He loves me so much that He would sacrifice his own Son for me, why didn't he save them and rescue me from this nightmare? Maybe He couldn't. As I struggled, I remembered the story of Job and how God allowed Job to suffer by taking his wife, his children, his home and everything he had. Job, too, struggled with questioning God. Again, I dug into God's Word for answers. If you have not dug into the story of Job, I challenge you to do so. It reveals much about God's love, His power, and that this life really isn't about us.

Ah, Sovereign Lord, you have made the Heavens and the earth by your great power and outstretched arm. Nothing is too hard for you.

Jeremiah 32:17

How do God's love and sovereignty work together? *If He loves me and had the power to put that plane with Larry and Landon safely on the ground, why didn't He?* I questioned, cried, and again I kept hearing God's whisper, "This isn't about you." I hated hearing that. Then God showed me His sacrifice. I knew God gave His Son as the ultimate sacrifice, but I had never thought about it in terms of my own suffering. You see, when I compare the two, would I have given up my child for the world? NO. I wouldn't have given up or sacrificed my own child for even my own mother. My love for my child exceeded all other love. How could God sacrifice His own Son for all of us... for me, an unfaithful, questioning, sinner who knows right from wrong and often chooses wrong. Because God knew the whole picture. He understood eternity and that this one sacrifice would bring countless others of His children to share eternity one day. As I began to wrap my head around this idea, I began to understand God's whisper, "This is not about you."

If this life is not about me, if I keep an eternal focus, then what do I do with all this pain? I write, I share, I speak, I live a life that honors HIM. I too will one day be reunited with my loved ones at the feet of Jesus. Until then, my life is not about me. My job is to love others and help them survive the unimaginable pain of loss.

But do not forget this one thing, dear friends: With the Lord a day is like a thousand years, and a thousand years are like a day.

———————

2 Peter 3:8

November 15, 2014

3 months... Sadness,
loneliness, despair, apathy
grief, missing them, anger.
The list goes on and on.
My life has been so
drastically changed as my
child was ripped from
this life while I was
left here to grieve. Its
overwhelming and heartbreaking
Its so lonely. I struggle
with bed time because that
is when we snuggled. I
would hold him tight.
We would wrap our
arms around each
other and fall asleep
content we were in the

arms of our most loved.
It's so hard to grieve
Larry with the overwhelmingly
sad loss of Landon.
I love him so much.
I love them both and
miss them. I don't know
how to move on without
Landon. Larry I
understand. I understand
falling in love and finding
a companion. I don't
know how to be content
after losing my child.
I can never have that
type of love again.

The Lord is faithful to all His promises and loving toward all He has made.
Psalm 145:13

12
Chapter

Faith Challenged

Faith is personal. My survival is all about a personal and very intimate relationship with my Heavenly Father. It's as personal as being a wife and a mom was. It takes daily time, effort, and commitment. My time, effort and commitment do not mean I understand or even admit to agreeing with God and His choices, but it has deepened my faith in a way that I really can't even explain. It's led me to intimately know my Heavenly Father and His love for me. It's led me to trust even when I don't understand. It allows me to know that my God is big enough and strong enough to handle all my doubts, my anger, my questions, and yet there is still no condemnation. It allows me to be comforted by Him in my weakest, darkest moments.

It wasn't always this way. Losing Larry and Landon challenged my faith to its core and in every way possible. All throughout this journey, as friends and loved ones were trying to comfort me, they would make statements like, "It's God's will." "This is God's plan." "God has you." "God will carry you through this" These comments infuriated me. First, I was just angry at God and then I began to doubt Him.

As I lay in bed at night crying, I would think, *How could God love me and allow this to happen? or If God is omnipotent, or all powerful, why didn't He keep them safe?* I really questioned God's sovereignty, meaning He has complete authority as Lord over creation and He exercises that power. How, then, could God send His Son to give His life for me, but then allow Larry and Landon to be taken from me? How can that much love, that much power, and that much pain all exist together? In my grief, it just couldn't, so I began to doubt all that my faith was built upon. I questioned it all.

To say I became angry with God is an understatement. I hated God for what had happened, but at the same time I would cry out to Him for comfort. I would spend hours contemplating my faith, God's Word, God's promises, prayer, and everything I thought to be true. Yet at the moments I felt most alone, I found myself talking to Him. This internal mental, emotional, spiritual conflict was exhausting. I decided to dive in and figure this out. I had to try to understand if God was indeed real.

I didn't know how to begin, so I read. The story that I kept remembering was Job, as I said earlier. I had grown up hearing about Job, but I'm not sure I ever read it for myself or studied Job. I knew that he had lost his home, servants, children, wealth, and health and never questioned God. Or so I thought. As you read, it is clear Job was in great pain. He cried out, *"Your hands shaped me and made me. Will you now turn and destroy me?"* Job 10:8 *"God assails me and tears me in his anger and gnashes his teeth at me;"* Job 16:9. Job was miserable and begged God to take his life, however, Job never denied Christ.

There was a time, after losing Larry and Landon, when I wondered what I had done to deserve this pain. I questioned why I was being punished. What great sin had I committed to justify this punishment? I relived in my mind all the great sins I had committed. I would contemplate each one, wondering why, regretting my choices, and still questioning God as to WHY? As I read in Job, I saw that Job's friends discussed that his suffering must be a result of his sin. Yet the Bible said Job feared God, shunned evil, and was blameless. It took a long time for me to come to terms that my loss was not punishment from God.

In the end, you see that Job never turns away from God, even through all his suffering. Job says, *"I know that you can do all things; no purpose of yours can be thwarted. You asked, 'Who is this that obscures my plans without knowledge?' Surely I spoke of things I did not understand, things too wonderful for me to know."* Job 42: 2-3 That's the thing about faith. Sometimes we just have to accept and no longer question. No matter where I was in my faith, my God was big enough to handle it. Even when I cursed God, even when I thought I hated God, even amid every doubt of His power, love and sovereignty, God was faithful. He truly is big enough, powerful enough, loving enough, and forgiving enough to handle all my doubts and questions.

Throughout all this struggle with faith I decided two things: One, it's all about perspective. I have to keep a Heavenly and eternal perspective. If I stay focused on my pain and trials of this life, it's easy to feel sorry for myself and get stuck. In contrast, when I have a Heavenly eternal perspective, I can be thankful for my nine-and-a-half years with Landon and my 22 years with Larry. When I stay Heavenly and eternally focused, I realize that this life is just a vapor in time. When I stay Heavenly and eternally focused, I realize that I will meet them again at the feet of my Heavenly Father. When I am Heavenly and eternally focused, I realize that God will wipe away all my tears and take away all my pain.

Two, this life is not about me. This thought is intricately intertwined with having a Heavenly eternal perspective. Throughout my grief I heard God's constant whisper that this life is not about me. I had to dig deep to discover and remind myself why God created people and why He created me. It was…and is, all about a relationship with Him and eternity with Him. And sometimes God crosses that line and awful things happen to good people like me so that other people can come to know Him.

Jesus said to her, 'I am the resurrection and the life. The one who believes in me will live, even though they die; and whoever lives by believing in me will never die. Do you believe this?'

John 11:25-26

Charlotte Liptack

I read this often. I know it in my head, yet my heart is broken and needs to be reminded. There were and are times where I must remind myself of this daily. We must remember that our brains are logical and our hearts are emotional. They do not speak the same language. This is why so many people of faith struggle after loss. My head knows that I will see Larry and Landon again in eternity and for all eternity. My heart misses them more than words can explain. Sometimes the pain is so overwhelming it's even hard to pray. But I know God can handle my brokenness if I just lay it at His feet. In those moments when I can't even mutter a prayer over the tears, I simply cry, "Jesus, Jesus, Jesus," over and over. Without fail, every single time, God provides a peace I cannot explain. I simply know He is there.

13
Chapter

When The Sublime Is Ripped from Our Grasp

Although I was a wife who lost my husband on the same day I lost my son, the grief just doesn't compare. There is no doubt that my grief for my son overshadowed that for my husband. In fact, it was over a year of grieving and dealing with the intense pain of losing my son before I even began to grieve for my husband. It may seem harsh but it is my reality. My grief had to be compartmentalized to survive it. I only know of a few people who lost both spouse and child at the same time and they have shared the same feelings.

Recently, a grieving mother who lost her five-year-old son to cancer asked me how to survive Mother's Day. I wept as I read her text and tried to respond, thinking and grieving for my own child. Mother's Day and Father's Day are some of the most difficult and bittersweet holidays for those of us who have lost our children. Bittersweet because there is no greater joy than the blessing of parenthood and no greater sorrow than losing that child.

Society has a word for a child who has lost a parent, orphan. There is a word for a man or woman who has lost a spouse, widow or widower. There is even a word for a spouse who has left another, divorcee. There is no known word, in any language, for the parent who is left after a child has died. Is it because it is so unnatural, or is it because no word is adequate?

As I typed a response to my friend, I reflected on my own loss and how I try to continue to survive. There were a few things I shared that come to mind:

God knows our pain. Yes, God lost his only Son. He watched from Heaven as Jesus was tortured and crucified. He did this all so I can have eternity with Him. There is comfort in knowing that my Creator and Heavenly Father understands, and at the same time, because of this great sacrifice, this is not the end. One day we will reunite with our children and wipe away all our tears.

Our grief is so overwhelmingly intense because our love is so big. I used to tell my son, "I love you to the moon and back a zillion infinities." I'm not sure how big that really is but my love (yes, present tense love) is even bigger than that. We don't stop loving just because they aren't in our arms or within eyesight. We keep loving, we keep missing, therefore we keep grieving. Grief for a child is forever, with time, it just gets a little easier to breathe.

God cherishes the parent-child relationship. Joseph and Mary were chosen and honored. The Bible talks about both of Jesus' parents with such admiration. I know that we are created as eternal beings and once a mom, always a mom, for all eternity. I certainly have no idea what Heaven looks like, but I imagine that one day in Heaven I get to be a "mom" to my son again. I can't wait for that day.

Mother's Day and Father's Day are just hard days. Whether you have other children like my friend, or lost your only child, like me, it will be difficult. I try to stay busy on each of those days. For me, I need things to be different than they used to be. I consume myself with activities and find some small way to honor my child. It's usually private, sometimes by design, but often because others are off celebrating their own mothers and children. There is no right or wrong answer, it's just what feels right. With time, the storm of grief will be a little less intense on those days.

Jesus said, "Let the little children come to me, and do not hinder them, for the kingdom of Heaven belongs to such as these."

Matthew 19:14

I was at a conference and a keynote was speaking on positive energy and being a positive person, however, when she referred to negative people and negative energy, she referred to grief. In fact, three different times she referred to grief as a negative quality. She grouped "grief" with other negative characteristics like apathy, anger, and fear. I'm assuming she may not have experienced life-changing grief like that of the loss of child, spouse or parent. I also know she never meant to be offensive; overall it was a great message. I'm still perplexed as to why we view grief so negatively.

Never let anyone tell you that your grief is negative. It's a part of you and your story. It's a journey and a roadmap of where we have been. I will say that how we handle our grief can be positive or negative. If it paralyzes us, defines us, or imprisons us in fear, it is certainly negative, but we can use our grief in beautiful, positive ways to inspire, motivate, encourage, help and change.

I also know that it takes magnificent people to love us with our grief. It's too hard for a lot of people. Sadly, there were those who couldn't stand with me. Only the strongest, most faithful, and secure individuals can love, support, and hold those of us who have big grief.

My grief is an expression of my love. I grieve deeply because I loved so deeply. My grief is big because my love was monumental. My grief is emotional because my love was passionate. My grief is never-ending because my love is eternal. My grief is wholehearted because my love was unconditional. My grief is beautiful because my love was magnificent.

November 1, 2014
Landon,
     I never loved anyone as
much as I loved you. You
were the only thing I ever
did so perfectly. You were
absolutely beautiful and
perfect in my eyes. It breaks

Live a life of love, just as Christ loved us and gave Himself up for us as a
fragrant offering and sacrifice to God.
Ephesians 5:2

my heart that I can never hold you in my arms again. I loved snuggling you. How will I ever be ok again after losing you. God says He loves you even more than I do. I can't imagine that but it gives me comfort as I know you are perfectly happy and comforted by both your heavenly and earthly father. I think of you every day all through out the day. You will always be my perfect little boy. I love you. I wish I could hold you. You are my heart forever.

Love, Mom

"You will call upon Me and come and pray to Me, and I will listen to you.
You will seek Me and find Me when you seek Me with all your heart."
Jeremiah 29:12-13

14
Chapter

The Beautiful, Ugly Truth

The truth is that grief is downright ugly. I have cried countless tears and still do. I have cursed God, yelled at God, told God He was a liar and that there was no way He really loved me. I have laid on the shower floor crying until the water turned cold, only then to crawl to the bathroom floor and cry some more. I have been on my knees screaming at God with tears running down my face, snot pouring out of my nose, hyperventilating and barely able to breathe, just begging God for this nightmare to end and for none of it to be true. At least 100 times I have asked God to trade my life for someone else's so they could stay with their family. During these past eight years, there have been times I have felt helpless, hopeless, unloved, alone, and completely lost. I have met God in the darkest places of wanting to end my own life.

Yet through all of this, God has been faithful. On those cold, lonely nights laying on the bathroom floor, God wrapped His arms around me in a blanket of warmth I could tangibly feel, and whispered that He was there to carry me. He sent angels to encourage me in those darkest moments. He has shown up to calm my anxiety when I couldn't utter a prayer through the sobs. He continues to hold me, carry me, encourage me, and provide more than I could have ever hoped for. And when I finally found contentment with being alone, He blessed me.

The ugly truth is, time does not heal all wounds. With time, I only learned to cope better. Eight years later, grief can still hit me like an unexpected downpour. It can wash over me when I see a boy and his mom, when I hear, "I love you," during a TV commercial, driving down the road listening to music, watching a sunset, or even with a sweet scent. It threatens my joy, my happiness, and my peace. Love, though, intercedes. It fills the voids. It solidifies my HOPE and reminds me that this world, this life, are just a twinkle in eternity.

God's healing, love and peace have taken many forms; they have come in the form of friends and family, the angels He sends, His Word, the calls of birds, the beauty of a sunset, the majesty of the mountains, the splendor of the sea, in the grace of others, and in the crepe myrtle that blooms purple and white. Grief is ugly, but the healing is beautiful; it's the beautiful, ugly truth.

October 19, 2014

I often feel like I'm drowning in this grief. I've lost parts of myself that define me. I'm a widow and a childless mother. The parts of me that are gone still long to be a mother and wife. How do I define myself? I don't want a new life. I want my old life, the one that was stolen. This emptiness is overwhelming. I don't want to survive it. I don't want to kill myself; I just don't want to keep living. I often pray for God to take me. It makes me sound crazy to pray for

these things. I pray for
cancer, a tumor, a disease,
an accident, a heart
attack, anything that will
take me out of this world
and into heaven.

No doubt I've changed. I
seek God more. I pray.
I'm in His presence. I
want to follow His will.
I appreciate people more.
I value and don't take for
granted the important
relationships in my life. I'm
waiting for God's plan for
greatness and joy.

I'm ready for my
sleepover friends to go home.
I'm ready for some independence.
I'm ready for real healing.

I trust in Your unfailing love. I will rejoice because You have rescued me.
I will sing to the LORD because He has been so good to me.
Psalm 13:5-6

The problem is I don't know how to start healing. I'm not sure how to grieve. It's too painful. I only know I miss my son and husband. I'm lonely and in pain.

God,
Please help me to heal. Show me how to grieve. Help me surround myself with family and friends who will keep praying and help me to find my "New Normal". Please just help the pain to subside. Help my heart not hurt so much.

Live a life of love, just as Christ loved us and gave Himself up for us as a fragrant offering and sacrifice to God.
Ephesians 5:2

15
Chapter

A Worthy Journey

Webster's dictionary defines to HOPE as "to want something to happen or be true," or "to desire with expectation of obtainment or fulfillment." I would argue that Webster missed the mark regarding true HOPE.

There was a day not too many years ago when I had to make a very conscious and active decision to either keep living life or to give up. I decided I would trust God's plan and keep living life. I was only able to make that decision because of HOPE, and I know HOPE isn't a wish or a desire. **True HOPE is an absolute faith and certainty of God and His promises.** No matter how much I wished tragedy had not struck, it still had. No matter how much I desired to have my child back in my arms, it would not happen. There was no amount of wishing or desiring that could have changed the outcome. However, HOPE in God's promises grounded my faith. My HOPE was grounded in the knowledge that this life isn't about me; it's about furthering the kingdom of God. It's also grounded in God's love, His forgiveness, His sacrifice, and an eternity with Him. HOPE allows me to rest in the assurance that one day I will experience true peace in Heaven at the feet of my Savior and all my heartache, pain and sorrow will forever disappear. Because of my faith and HOPE, I know that my loved ones will be there, as well, and that our reunion will be more amazing than I can ever imagine. I've been at that place where life seems too difficult to continue. I've been in stormy waters and felt like I was drowning. You may be there as well. No matter how big the storm feels, how fast the waves are crashing, or how hard the wind is blowing, you too can rest in HOPE. You can cast all your worries, doubts, heartaches, and grief at the feet of our Jesus.

Therefore I tell you, do not worry about your life, what you will eat or drink; or about your body, what you will wear. Is not life more than food, and the body more than clothes? Look at the birds of the air, they do not sow or reap or store away in barns, and yet your Heavenly Father feeds them. Are you not much more valuable than they?

––––––––––––

Matthew 6: 25-26

I wish I could suggest an easy fix or prescription, but I can't. This is all much easier said than done. Immediately after the accident that took my husband and son, I was utterly overwhelmed with grief. I was consumed with pain and didn't know how I could survive this heartache. I worried about how I was going to get up and function and life with such deep pain. I worried about how I would do life alone without them. I worried about finances, taking care of the house, the outcome of the lawsuits, and taking care of others. Worry overcame me during this time.

At some point I had to remember that none of this life mattered, that I was a child of God, and He had all of this in the palm of His hand. I still find ways to worry about my life, my future and the plans God has for me. When that happens, I simply call out the name of Jesus and He is always faithful to comfort me. Frequently, as I take it back and worry, I still have to give it all back to Him. Learning how to HOPE is not easy, but it is a central part of a worthy journey on the road to healing and life.

After a friend of mine recently lost her husband, she asked me how I got through it and how to survive. She asked something that I often thought, "This is painful, how do I get through grief more quickly so I'm not in such awful pain?" I had this thought so often. The pain of losing my husband and son was so intense I couldn't breathe. I so badly wanted to move through grief and get to the other side. Unfortunately, grief takes time and I'm not sure there is another side. Because we loved deeply, we will forever grieve, but we do heal. Healing is a long journey and this is all about the journey, not the destination. What I did learn are ways to facilitate healing.

Believe - First and foremost, you must believe that you are a child of God's and that He understands and loves all your dysfunctional mess. You also must believe in healing and in HOPE. I knew without a doubt I was a child of the King. I knew my eternity was sealed, and I would spend it in Heaven. What I didn't know was if I could really be healed in this life. I assumed I would always be as miserable and heartbroken if I lived on this earth, but shortly after losing my loved ones I received a book from a friend, Dori Phillips. She lost her husband and several of her children in a traffic automobile accident. In her book A Love Greater Than Death she talks about believing in healing. She shared her journey and I began to believe that I too could be healed. When I began to believe in healing I began to feel the weight of grief being lifted.[1]

Belongings - About three months after the accident, I was driving through downtown Houston on my way to a football game. On my route, there were numerous homeless individuals living on the streets. Many were shivering and cold. I remember thinking about the closet full of both Larry's and Landon's clothes. I thought to myself that if something happened to me, I would want someone who needed my things to have them. It was at that moment I knew I had to sort through their personal belongings. This was a lot easier said than done. It was gut-wrenching, painful work. I wept over each garment, toy, and personal item. I sniffed anything I could find, desperately searching for just a scent of them. Back and forth I changed my mind thousands of times about what I would donate and what I would keep. In

---

[1] Phillips, Dori. *A Love Greater Than Death*. *Houston*, CreateSpace Independent Publishing, 2011

the end, that task was incredibly healing. It's something that is necessary and helps move you to and through a place you are reluctant to go. How and when you decide to go through belongings, get support. There were many times I had to stop, walk away, shut the door, fall apart, and get support before I could re-engage in the process. While going through belongings, I found the things that mattered most, and found beautiful ways to create lifelong heirlooms out of those belongings. It's a tough but necessary part of the journey. As harsh as it sounds, it helps us to internalize the finality.

Beginnings - It's necessary to start new traditions, to begin to do things differently, and to figure out who you are outside of your loved ones. About three months after the accident, I was bombarded with my son's birthday, a week later, Thanksgiving, and three weeks after that, Christmas. I knew these milestones would be tough, but what I didn't expect was the tidal wave of feelings that would accompany the loss of traditions. Assuming I could still engage in some of those traditions was naïve. I thought it would bring me some sort of comfort, but instead, engaging intensified the pain. Through the years, I'm beginning to find ways to navigate through special days and holidays. I don't think it matters what you do or who you do it with, as long as you find a way to find joy and celebrate memories throughout your journey.

Breathe - Finally, it's important to stop often, breathe, and reflect on the journey. Taking time to read over old journals reminds me of how amazingly far I have come. It's sometimes so hard to see the progress, especially when I'm weighted down in the sorrow of missing them. It's so important to occasionally find time alone to do this. My new favorite way to do this is scuba diving. It's perfectly peaceful and a beautiful connection to God where I can do nothing but breathe, praise, and pray. Find your place to just stop and breathe. It doesn't have to be far away or for long periods of time. Before diving, it was in my closet or in the shower. Just find a place alone to breathe.

This is what the Sovereign Lord says to these bones: I will make breath enter you, and you will come to life.

Ezekiel 37:5

Be still, (just breathe) and know that I am God.

Psalms 46:10

For I know the plans I have for you," declares the LORD, "plans to prosper you and not to harm you, plans to give you hope and a future.

Jeremiah 29:11

We have this HOPE as an ANCHOR for the soul, firm and secure. *It enters the inner sanctuary behind the curtain where our forerunner, Jesus, has entered on our behalf.*

Hebrews 6:19-20

December 28, 2015

As this year draws to a close I have to reflect. I really can see the healing in so many ways:

1) I can write about my life without crying.
2) I can see that God wants me to share this story for His glory.
3) I'm willing to tell the story to help others.
4) I can talk about Landon without falling apart.
5) I can talk about Larry and not be angry.
6) I'm ready to be happy again.

My soul finds rest in God alone; my salvation comes from Him.
Psalm 62:1

7) I find joy in some activities and some people.

8) I look forward to things like DC, San Francisco, Spring break.

9) I enjoy relationships.

10) I want to help others.

11) I'm open to God's purpose for my life.

11) I'm writing again

12) I no longer pray for God to take me.

13) I want to live and not just survive.

14) I can express a lot of different emotions.

15) I want to love and be loved again

16
Chapter

Lean In

The thing about grief is, you can't run from it. It will eventually catch you. I used to search for how to move through it more quickly. You can't run from it, you can't just get past it, you can't move through it more quickly; you must take the journey one day at a time and sit with the grief. There are times you will see it coming at you like a slow, gentle wave and you can brace for the waters. Other times it's like a torrent that you never see coming and it devastates all in its path. Regardless, you must ride out the wave or devastation; it can't be avoided.

Grief is the deep sorrow caused by a loved one's death. Grieving is the process of learning to live with that deep pain and loss. The more you loved, the deeper your suffering when you lose the one you loved. Throughout my healing these past years I've learned some things. This insight, although mostly based on experience, has also come from my years of training as a Licensed Professional Counselor and research from so many who are grieving.

- Lean into grief. There is no wrong or right way to grieve, as long as you aren't hurting yourself or others. Make no mistake, your emotions will often get the better of you and you will make a lot of mistakes that sometimes-hurt others. Just remember to keep communicating. I found myself apologizing a lot those first few years. Those who love me are gracious and forgiving and always give me space to grieve how I need.

- Lean in on friends. It's a lonely road, but you don't have to travel it alone. It's true that no one can help you grieve. No one will truly understand your pain with all the complexities that were part of your relationship and your life. You can allow others, especially those who have walked this road, to take the journey with you. It's one of the hardest roads you will ever take, so why not lean on others? It's important to have close confidants with whom you can share your concerns, fears, heartache, healing, and even ask for prayer and support. It's downright foolish not to use your support network.

- Lean in on healing. Relationships are hard, especially while grieving. Don't start new romantic relationships while grieving. I had so many people warn me about this, and all my own training supports this idea. The same part of your heart that loves is the part that grieves. It's simply impossible to start a romantic relationship with someone while grieving. It's often hard to just hold on to the existing relationships, spouses, significant others, let alone start a new relationship, but loneliness often gets to people and they reach for companionship. The problem is, no matter how much people want to, they can't understand the depths of your pain, yet engage in a healthy relationship and get what they need to move forward. Resentment and hurt are always the result. I absolutely knew better and still walked down that road; I have personally experienced this more than once. Healing must happen first. Give yourself some grace here and save yourself some heartache. Depend on good friends, give yourself at least a year to heal, devote your time and energy into your own heart, strengthening your faith and your relationship with God.

- Lean in and be patient. Don't rush! Give yourself plenty of time to go through all the stages of grief. There is no order, there is no timeline, there is only you and your heart. If you slow down, rely on your faith and strength, pray and meditate, read and learn, and just breathe, then you will know how to deal with each of the stages. No matter what stage you are in, just be present. Whether you are in denial, sad, lonely, angry, mad, helpless, depressed, anxious, or even beginning to accept, just sit with it until you feel like you've thoroughly processed it and are ready to let it go.

- Lean in on sharing and service. Last, and most important, I will say just lean in. In the best way you know how, just lean in on everything you are feeling and then find something good to do with it. There is a world full of hurting people. There are others who desperately need your survival story. People need to hear your story and all of the hardship along your journey. Don't be afraid to share and be a blessing to someone else who is grieving. We are created to LOVE. There is nothing else more important than what we pour into others. There has been nothing more healing for my soul than helping others. I believe that one day we will all stand to account for that love and I want to hear, "Well done, my good and faithful servant!"

July 27, 2016

I love reading God's word.
It is my strength. It
encourages me, fills me up,
guides me and pulls me out of
this dark place.

I received a facebook
challenge from my friend
Christina Rice to post scripture
every day for 7 days. I
needed that. I needed to
read. I loved reading
everyone else scriptures as
well. I've been i such
a crazy emotional funk
lately. Its been so hard
to get up and just function
every day. Why? ~~toto~~ How
is it while you are healing

The LORD is my strength, my shield from every danger.
I trust in Him with all my heart.
Psalm 28:7

you can have a relapse and struggl again. I've often criticized others for being so emotional and yet I am so overly emotional and sensitive lately. "They" are right. Karma is a bitch.

Healing is interesting. It doesn't happen on its own. You have to be intentional purposeful and diligent in healing.

Here are things I know I have to do daily to heal and continue healing.

1) Read God's word and books/stories of others healing. So many others have traveled this road. There is so much to learn

In Him we have redemption through His blood,
the forgiveness of sins, in accordance with the riches of God's grace.
Ephesians 1:7

from others. God's word
is a guide a well. God
himself mourned Jesus.
. 2) Prayer. This is the
most essential. Often
I find myself simply
calling out the name of
Jesus over and over again.
Mostly when I'm
broken and its the only
I can find the strength
to say or do. Sometimes I
can really pray and
tell God how I feel. I
know he knows but it feels
good to just say it.
3) Talk to others and tell
them what you need. This
one is really hard for me.
How do I ask? Why do I
ask? I know people get

tired of hearing about my pain and suffering. I'm so afraid of running them off. I me However, its necessary. Journaling can be that as well.

④ Finally just <u>cry</u> and release. Its a mature part of release and its beneficial in so many ways.

Live a life of love, just as Christ loved us and gave Himself up for us as a
fragrant offering and sacrifice to God.
Ephesians 5:2

17
Chapter

Peace Under the Surface

There is absolutely nothing normal about my "new normal." Since the accident, my two beautiful stepdaughters have given birth to my three beautiful step-grandchildren. I can't imagine life without them. I wish Larry and Landon were here to experience the joy they bring. Landon would have been a cool uncle and Larry would have been the best Papa on the earth, no doubt.

I decided life was too short to keep doing what I was doing. I retired early, sold my house in the Houston area and began to travel and enjoy scuba diving. After losing Larry and Landon, I struggled to find peace. Actually, let me say, I still struggle. It's a daily choice to live in peace. But finding the places that allow me to live in and experience that tranquility has been a journey. What I discovered within just a few weeks was that nature is where I felt closest to God, peace, and my boys. Being outside was where I could begin to let go of some of my fears, anxiety and grief. About a year after they died, I decided to take up scuba diving. It's something Larry and I had often talked about. It's been a truly magical experience. Finally, I truly felt I had found absolute peace and tranquility the first time I descended beneath the surface of the water.

There is no doubt that there is a little build up to the dive. You plan, prep, and get your gear ready. Like anticipating any activity, you know it's coming, you can't wait, but you never quite anticipate just how joyous it will be. The boat ride out to the reef is very relaxing, and if possible, I begin to get my mind ready. Once there I suit up, jump in the water, and wait for the divemaster to say, "Let's go down." You don't know this, but I smile every time I hear those words. I quickly release the air from my BCD, the buoyancy control device you wear, and begin my descent below the surface.

From the moment my ears fall below the surface I'm at peace. Immediately, all noise is shut out. I can hear only my own breath. I often shut my eyes those first few moments as I equalize my ears and focus on my steady breathing. Slowly my descent relaxes every fiber of my body. The weightlessness allows my muscles to relax, especially those in my neck and shoulders where I carry every bit of stress and anxiety. After less than a minute my eyes open and I'm totally in the moment. I take long deep breaths in and then slowly release every worry, every care, every anxiety, and every fear (at least for the next 60-75 minutes). Diving in Cozumel is one of my favorites because of the current. I can just be still and take it all in. The world below the surface is mostly unscathed by the world above. There are no politics, no electronics, no divisiveness, no hate, no voices, no distractions, no noise, only the sound of my own breath and the bubbles as I exhale. I experience a part of creation that many never see. The world below the surface moves with the ebb and flow of the ocean in perfect harmony. I have no task or chore when under the water; I'm simply an observer. The colors are spectacular, the abundant life is exhilarating, the reef in contrast to the deep blue is just breathtaking. Like a sunset, I just can't get enough of the view. I don't think under the water; I'm sure that is part of why it's so peaceful. I only concentrate on the beautiful creation, my breathing, the feeling of weightlessness and letting go. Throughout the dive I occasionally snap a photo to share with those who never get to experience life below. I regularly check my dive watch and my air pressure, and in the words of Dorie, "just keep swimming" and soaking in the warm, salty water, the view, the tranquility of it all.

I used to begin to get a little anxious when it was time to ascend. I'm not sure what all of that was about, anxiety of a safety stop or sadness the dive was ending. Anyways, now I've found my peace in the ascension and safety stop. If you were to see me at the safety stop, it looks like I'm dialed into deep concentration staring at my computer as it counts down. I take those last five minutes and simply thank God for the opportunity. I quit observing and I'm simply still, physically, emotionally, mentally, and spiritually. I find praise in the moment, I reminisce about all I've encountered, I thank God I am here and have survived such tragedy, I continue to listen to my breath, and meditate as I cherish every second under water.

Webster's dictionary says peace is "a state of tranquility or quiet; freedom from disquieting or oppressive thoughts or emotions." The Bible says, *"Peace I leave with you; my peace I give you. I do not give to you as the world gives. Do not let your hearts be troubled and do not be afraid."* John 14:27.

No matter where you are in life, it's important to have true peace. Find the place that allows you freedom from all the distractions of the world. Discover what activity and where you allow yourself to release all the anxiety and worry. Find your tranquility!

18
Chapter

Healing 3/31/21

I write this final chapter almost 7 years after the accident. I'm sitting on an airplane traveling back from an eight-month trip in Cozumel, Mexico. It's truly the pinnacle in my healing. When I arrived in Cozumel, I had been on a journey of healing but had never truly accepted being alone. Consequently, I had a few bad relationships; I stayed in abusive, unhealthy situations out of fear of being alone. I knew I had to face being alone and there was no better way to do that than heading to a foreign country and truly living life alone.

Although I would say I am an extremely spiritual person, I didn't truly have peace about my loss. Everyone knows the song, "It is well with my soul." I've heard it in church often these past seven years but refused to sing it. This life I was living was NOT well with my soul.

When I arrived in Cozumel, I had never even been to a restaurant alone. I vowed to myself to dive like crazy and go out alone every night and meet people. In between, I would meditate, pray, reflect, remember, and find MY inner joy. I would embrace my being alone. I knew I could never really share life with someone, love someone, give my heart to someone, until I gave myself this gift of healing and being content alone.

To commit, I paid the eight months' rent up front. I'm not going to lie, my first several weeks were tough. Many times, I questioned this decision and wanted to get on a plane and go back home. But I persisted in my pursuit to find myself. I shed many tears along the way. Slowly but surely, I began to settle in and find true peace.

When I wasn't diving, I was in the water. I would daily walk three blocks to the ocean, jump in, and let the cool, salty waters rush over my skin. It felt like it would wash the stress and insecurities away and daily cleanse my soul. The ocean is magical that way. Each evening, I would sit on the sea wall and watch the sunset. I would reflect on the day, embrace my healing, and watch God paint this beautiful portrait of the sun setting across the ocean. I would sit with myself for hours in these moments and reminisce, reflect, accept, and allow myself to be still and quiet. I've always loved sunsets, but now they have new meaning. Sunsets were where my heart began to heal, where I found peace in being alone, and where I once again began to allow my heart to love. Sunsets allowed me to reflect on my growth and my journey for that day. It is also a beautiful reminder of a new dawn and new HOPE and that I get to start again tomorrow. Finally, it's the perfect picture proof that endings can be beautiful.

No matter your loss, there can be healing on the other side. It is a choice; It's a daily choice to heal and it's a daily choice to find light, beauty, happiness, and peace in all situations. I still don't have answers as to why God took my husband and child home, but I have a "peace that passes all understanding" and it's grounded in HOPE. I don't know all God has in store for me, but I can once again sing....

"When peace like a river attendeth my way
When sorrows like sea billows roll
Whatever my lot, Thou hast taught me to say
It is well, it is well with my soul."

"It Is Well With My Soul" is a hymn written by hymnist Horatio Spafford after suffering the tragic loss of his children.

About Kharis Publishing:

Kharis Publishing, an imprint of Kharis Media LLC, is a leading Christian and inspirational book publisher based in Aurora, Chicago metropolitan area, Illinois. Kharis' dual mission is to give voice to under-represented writers (including women and first-time authors) and equip orphans in developing countries with literacy tools. That is why, for each book sold, the publisher channels some of the proceeds into providing books and computers for orphanages in developing countries, so that these kids may learn to read, dream, and grow. For a limited time, Kharis Publishing is accepting unsolicited queries for nonfiction (Christian, self-help, memoirs, business, health, and wellness) from qualified leaders, professionals, pastors, and ministers. Learn more at: About Us - Kharis Publishing - Accepting Manuscript

CPSIA information can be obtained
at www.ICGtesting.com
Printed in the USA
BVHW041410280422
635622BV00017B/701

9 781637 461259